3:AM Kisses

A Novel

ADDISON MOORE

Other books by Addison Moore:

New Adult Romance

3:AM Kisses (3:AM Kisses 1)
Winter Kisses (3:AM Kisses 2)
Sugar Kisses (3:AM Kisses 3)
Whiskey Kisses (3:AM Kisses 4)
Rock Candy Kisses (3:AM Kisses 5)
Velvet Kisses (3:AM Kisses 6)
Someone to Love (Someone to Love 1)
Someone Like You (Someone to Love 2)
Someone For Me (Someone to Love 3)
Burning Through Gravity (Burning Through Gravity 1)
A Thousand Starry Nights (Burning Through Gravity 2)
Beautiful Oblivion (Beautiful Oblivion 1)
Beautiful Illusions (Beautiful Oblivion 2)
The Solitude of Passion
Celestra Forever After (Celestra Forever After 1)
The Dragon and the Rose (Celestra Forever After 2)
Perfect Love (A Celestra Novella)

Young Adult Romance

Ethereal (Celestra Series Book 1)
Tremble (Celestra Series Book 2)
Burn (Celestra Series Book 3)

ADDISON MOORE

Wicked (Celestra Series Book 4)
Vex (Celestra Series Book 5)
Expel (Celestra Series Book 6)
Toxic Part One (Celestra Series Book 7)
Toxic Part Two (Celestra Series Book 7.5)
Elysian (Celestra Series Book 8)
Ethereal Knights (Celestra Knights)
Ephemeral (The Countenance Trilogy 1)
Evanescent (The Countenance Trilogy 2)
Entropy (The Countenance Trilogy 3)

Prologue

Baya

Sometimes life has its way with you. It peels back the layers of your existence like the skin of an onion until the real you glows underneath, raw and painful to the touch. It's in those moments, in that hour, you look to those that give you strength—for me, that person was my brother. He was the one that put me on a pedestal after tragedy struck in our young lives. He promised to always look after me. To make sure that I wouldn't stumble in life and that the right people would land beside me along the way. It's no coincidence most of those people were of the estrogen card-carrying variety. My brother loves me so much he pinned me high on the good girl board long before I could have contested the effort, and, now that I'm admiring the view below, I'm not so sure I want to be the poster child for innocence anymore.

It's funny how something like death, which isn't funny at all, can shape your destiny. When my father was alive, all he talked about was his heyday at Whitney Briggs, and, of course, being little I imagined him stuck on a farm, pitching straw over his shoulder—but Whitney Briggs is a far cry from any countryside barn. Whitney

Briggs University is billed as a cosmopolitan educational institution tucked in the blue mountains of North Carolina, and, so, after he died, both my brother and I set our scholastic compass in that direction. That's where destiny kicks in, and I meet *him*.

Bryson Edwards. Even his name makes me sigh.

He's right here, and I want nothing more than to close the gap between us until he falls into me. I'm boiling over, ready to have him, ready for him to have me any way he wishes.

I stretch my arms up over my head and wriggle my body into his mattress.

His chest ticks with a silent laugh. "Whatever it is you're doing, keep doing it." A seam of moonlight catches his features, exposing the fact he clearly approves.

"I'm settling in." I twist my hips into the bed. "I think I could get a good night's sleep here."

"Oh, sweetie"—he growls it out as the smile slides off his face —"if you spent the night in my room, there wouldn't be a whole hell of a lot of sleeping going on." His fiery breath sears over my mouth like a promise. "And, if you did happen to fall asleep, I'd be guilty of doing something very, very wrong."

My fingers run down his granite-like abs and unbutton his jeans. I glide down the bed and plant a kiss just above his boxers.

"I don't plan on sleeping," I say it low like a threat. "And neither should you."

1

The Arrival

Baya

I'm pretty sure flashing your boobs at the hottest guy in a ten-mile radius isn't the best way to meet new friends on move-in day.

"Shit!" I pull my tube top up, quick as a flicker, but it doesn't matter, "the girls" have already made their startling debut right here in Founder's Square in front of a demigod who's witnessed the first of many embarrassing episodes I'm sure to have at Whitney Briggs. "I swear I don't know how that happened." I pluck and adjust, while struggling to hold onto the oversized duffle bag I've filled with all of my dad's favorite books. When he died I sort of adopted them, and, now, I'm dragging them around like a body. It was the one bag I didn't check and thankfully so since the airline sent the rest of my things to Kansas. "It's like a ghost just pulled it down. Stupid top."

"I don't think it's stupid." He gives a lopsided grin, and my insides squeeze tight. He's gorgeous, and built, and way the hell out of my league. "I think it's friendly."

He dips his gaze to my cleavage again as if waiting for a reprisal.

"It's not friendly, and neither am I." I take a step to the left, and he's quick to block my path. "Look, sorry about the peep show. My clothes usually don't make a habit of falling off in front of people." His caramel hair glows in the dappled sunlight. It looks glossy and slick, and it's all I can do to keep my fingers from running through it.

"Don't feel too bad—clothes everywhere have a habit of falling off in my presence. Especially the undergarment variety." He gives a cocky grin. "In fact, I double dog dare you to do it again."

Perfect. He's tanned, ripped, and evidently ready to dip his wick.

"I'm leaving now." I ditch around him and step into the swell of humanity. Girls in every level of undress scream and hug as if summer had somehow lasted a thousand years. Dozens of skateboards jet by, quick and lethal as bullets, as I struggle my way through the main thoroughfare. If I wasn't lugging around all my father's books, which have decidedly morphed into bricks, I might have actually enjoyed my first stroll through campus. I had seen snippets of it in the glossy brochures, but I've basically shown up at Whitney Briggs sight unseen. The first thing I noticed when the airport shuttle dropped me off is the fact the air is thinner in the mountains of North Carolina, much more than it ever was in Texas. Back home you could take a bite out of the heat, and here it feels like I'm filling my lungs with something just this side of helium.

A pair of bicycles zoom at me in either direction, and I squeeze my eyes shut in a passive effort to avoid the near collision. They whisk by, and I force my lids to open once again. I could use a serious nap right about now and maybe a defibrillator if I ever manage to trek across this overgrown scholastic terrain. Swear to God, this campus is uphill both ways. Whoever thought it was a good idea to plop a school on the side of a mountain must have been part billy goat.

"You need a hand?" It's the tanned, ripped, dip-wick willing and able with his half-cocked smile, and I'm sure he's got a half-cock in his pants to match. Just as I'm about to protest the idea, he swipes the duffle bag from me without the proper invite, not that my tired muscles are willing to fight him. "Which way you headed?"

"No really, it's okay." I try to snatch it back, and he swings it just out of reach. His muscles redefine themselves, and a series of lightly sketched tattoos track up over his biceps.

"I promise I won't say a word to your dorm sisters about 'nipplegate.'"

I suck in a quick breath.

"Nipplegate?" Crap. I'm not on campus five minutes, and already I've caused a quasi-political scandal of mammary proportions, not that my boobs are anything news worthy. "I'm in Prescott Hall." I sag into the idea of him schlepping my things. I bet he's secretly going to call me nipples each time he sees me. In fact, I'm sure he'll share this juicy tidbit with his lowlife friends, and I'll have to endure four long years listening to things like nips, the nippler, nipapolis, the rack, *gah*—the *nom* rack!

Just shit.

I scan the area for signs of my brother, but he's nowhere to be found. He's the reason I'm at Whitney Briggs to begin with. I miss him. He's been out of the house for three long years, and I'm dying to be near him again. Cole is my favorite person in the world, no offense to Mom who is also pretty great. But after Dad died, Cole really became so much more than a big brother. Once he left, I lived for his weekly phone calls, and now that I'll get to spend time with him every day, the idea brings tears to my eyes. He's that sweet.

"Prescott it is." The blonde duffle bag wielding demon leads us to an overgrown building that to my surprise is in close proximity and doesn't require mountain climbing gear to get to. On the lower level there's a packed café with a giant sign in the window that reads *Hallowed Grounds*. The smell of fresh brewed coffee transforms the vicinity into a nirvana-like heaven. He gives a sly smile as he walks alongside me, and a fire rips through my bones.

A breath gets caught in my throat at the sight of his pale grey eyes—stunning is the only word I can think to accurately describe them. He's watching me, heating my skin with his stare, and my cheeks catch fire being this lethally close to him. I move my gaze lower and note his bulging biceps with the beginnings of a tattoo peering out from under the sleeve of his T-shirt. Whoever this is, he's spent some serious time at the gym, or prison—or maybe the gym *in* prison.

"So you're a freshman?" He opens the door to the building with his back and nods me in first.

"What gave it away? My 'How to Survive Your First Year at University' handbook for dummies or my perky peach nipples?" I smart as we step into the waiting elevator. I punch in the third floor, and we start to float.

"Neither, but the perky peach nipples were a nice surprise. You really know how to brighten a guy's day." His teeth illuminate like a row of stars, and I blush a deeper shade of crimson.

I want to say they don't call me Baya *Brighton* for nothing but resist the lame joke at the expense of my surname.

His smile fades as he takes me in. There's a sadness hiding there beneath those lightning grey eyes, and I can't pinpoint where it might be coming from.

"You've just got that freshman look about you." His voice gravels it out low, like a secret. "You look sweet—yet to be tainted by the masses. Most of the girls around here eat frat boys for breakfast. You don't strike me as the man-eater type. You've got 'good girl' written all over you." He says it with a leer as if he's ready and willing to revoke my good girl visa. And the way my thighs are quivering, I'm not sure I'd mind.

God, he sounds just like Cole. If I hear what a "good girl" I'm supposed to be one more time, I'm going to hurl all over his shiny new tennis shoes. As much as I love my brother, I'm tired of him reminding me of what a little angel I am. Honestly, sometimes it feels as if Cole wants to keep me a little girl forever.

"Yeah, well, being a good girl is highly overrated." I should know. Much to Cole's approval, I am one.

We step out, and I follow the number on the doors all the way down the hall. Most of the doors are opened, exposing the fact girls are busy decorating their miniaturized abodes with wall decals and superfluous purchases from Bed, Bath, and Beyond. Music blares from a room to our right and a tall redhead stomps out and tapes a poster of a fuzzy white kitten over her door that reads, A, B, C, D, E, then below the fuzzy cute kitty, F.U.

"Nice," I say, glancing over at the demigod of moving day. "Looks like I'm not the only friendly one around here."

"That's Roxy." He leans in as he says it, and his warm cologne washes over me like a private heat wave. He smells good, clean like warm spices mixed with soap. His silver-blue eyes sear into mine, and an earthquake rolls through my body. "She's pretty nice on days that don't end in Y."

"Again, just like me." My throat runs dry, and it takes all of my effort to break our gaze. I step up to room 315 and pause. "Here I am." I pump my shoulders excited to be anywhere I might actually belong. After Dad died,

Mom uprooted us to Texas where I always felt a little out of place. But this is *college*—my dorm. I'm going to finally fit in. And I'll have a roommate. What could be better than that? I bet we'll be friends for life, closer than sisters. I've always secretly wanted a sister, not that I'd trade Cole for one. He's pretty amazing as far as big brothers go. But I'm desperately in need of a little estrogen in my life, someone to dish about boys at all hours of the night over a carton of Cherry "breakup" Garcia. Someone to peruse the Victoria's Secret catalog with while debating boy-shorts or thongs, someone who can really appreciate Green Goddess dressing for what it truly is—culinary perfection.

I unlock the door and swing it wide open for my duffle-bag-wielding friend, but Conan the Chivalrous demands I enter first. The room itself is smaller than a hiccup with twin beds on either side and not much else. A bare wall greets me on one side and on the other—

The comforter is moving, slow and lethargic, like there's a giant anaconda buried deep beneath it.

Oh God, my insides cinch with fear. I hate to break it to my new dorm sister, but I don't do snakes, or rats, or even some of those little beady-eyed purse puppies that have a propensity to growl at people. Then a tangle of limbs pop out from beneath the sheets. A heavy demonic moan escapes the tiny bed as a waterfall of blonde hair floats to the floor.

Oh God, she's going to be sick.

Just as I'm about to kick over the trashcan, a bare hairy ass hikes into the air, and her equally hairy legs bend in flexion. Oh wow, she's got some serious follicular issues, but I totally won't hold it against her. In fact, it makes me like her more. I bet the poor thing never wears a bikini. I had a friend in high school who actually had the misfortune of growing hair on her chest. She was well on her way to morphing into a baboon before junior year. It's just one of those freak things that nature unleashes on poor unsuspecting testosterone-riddled girls, and there's not a whole lot you can do about it other than wax yourself silly, and God knows that's a little piece of hell right there.

I take a step forward just as the comforter flops off the bed.

Gah! There's two of them! And one of them is a *boy*!

I watch in horror as the hairy ass bumps and grinds while beneath him a svelte blonde lets out a satisfying "*Oh yes! Oh yes, yes, yes!*"

"Oh no. Oh *no, no, no.*" My hand flies to my lips, my feet still rooted to the floor.

The hairy ass picks up his pace, and the girl's boobs flops back and forth as if they were waving hello.

"Oh my, God." I push my face in the dip-wick's rock hard chest and lose myself momentarily rubbing my cheek against him. Good God, he's skin over steel.

"Whoa," he says, lowering the duffle bag to the floor. "Maybe we should just get going for now." He presses his hand in the small of my back, and my spine electrifies as he ushers me into the hall. He closes the door behind him as his laughing eyes magnetize to mine. "Welcome to your first day of school, princess." He gives a crooked grin, and this time it makes me feel oddly safe like he's just rescued me from some sexual dungeon of perversion. "Bryson Edwards." He holds out a hand, strong and thick, and a part of me wants to bite down over his fingers then extricate them from my mouth in a sexual manner rather than shake them.

"Baya." It rasps from me just barely audible.

His fingers clasp over mine, his eyes seal themselves over my features, pulling me in as if rescuing me from the deepest end of the ocean.

"Baya." He gives a brief nod, and that veiled sadness returns to his eyes. "Beautiful name for a beautiful girl." He leans in. A look of seduction sweeps over him. "Why don't I get you out of here."

I give a coy smile up at his blond eminence. "I double dog dare you."

ಬಿಜಿಪಿ

The temperature outside feels as if it's just dropped twenty degrees. Of course, it might have something to do with the fact I was sweating all the way down in the elevator while visions of my dorm room being defiled swirled in my head. Talk about your first day trauma and drama. As if the fact my boobs insisted on taking a look around campus wasn't bad enough—although technically my new roommate showed me up in the boob drama department. She was large and in charge, and, holy shit, those things were spinning out of control like hands on some demonic clock.

Right about now I'm starting to lose any sisterly connection I was feeling toward my new roommate. Her inability to blush while busting a move has quickly relegated her to more of a distant slutty cousin who I'm not opposed to removing.

I take in a lungful of air trying to cleanse my mind from the sight, but that hairy ass haunts me behind my lids, and, now, it'll forever be locked in my subconscious, taunting me as it bounces into the air. Crap. I can never un-see that.

A tall row of pines campaign for my attention. I choose to ignore the fact I just threw up a little in the back of my mouth and force myself to take in the scenery. The evergreens spear out like skyscrapers all along the outline of campus, and their sweet perfume infiltrates my senses.

"You want to grab some coffee?" Bryson cinches a smile and moves in close as we traverse an entire minefield of bicycles. My father loved to ride. He died that way, too. I try not to think about it, but, with my mind buzzing a million miles an hour, nothing seems off limits today.

"Coffee?" I pause to gaze up at Bryson's eyes, the exact shade of the pale sky and my toes curl at the sight of him. A brief vision of him raking his naked body over mine, moaning in my ear with passion, blinks through my mind, grey and fuzzy like a bad cable connection. He's so stunningly gorgeous, and, for the most part, gorgeous guys don't have too much to do with me. I'm guessing my boobs cast some sort of nipple spell on him, and now he thinks a homerun is in the works by midnight. For all I know he's got some boob fetish he's looking to satisfy. "I'd better not. I need to find my brother. I've texted him like six times since I got here, and he's pretty much ignored me which isn't like him." I'm more than a little worried, but I'm guessing he dropped his phone in the toilet or left it at home and went for a hike.

I spin in a slow circle trying to orient myself. The tall Gothic-style buildings give this place that Hogwarts' vibe I've always secretly craved, and the pepper trees, the weeping willows, the overgrown maples only lend to the magic. "I think I'll head over to the Briggs Apartment building. That's where he's staying. His name is Cole Brighton, have you heard of him?"

His head ticks back a notch. "Cole?" A tiny smile tugs at his lips. They look full and soft, and I bet kissing them would feel like falling into a bed of clouds—erotic, cocky clouds—nevertheless, he's still way out of my league. "Everyone knows Cole. I'm headed that way." He lands his hand over my shoulder, and my skin sizzles. "I'll take you right to him."

"Really? Thank you!" Everyone knows Cole, huh? I'm not sure why my brother's popularity surprises me. Cole is the nicest, most noble, decent guy on the planet. And now I'm suddenly thrilled to have bumped into Mr. Muscles here because he's going to take me right to him.

"You know, you're proving yourself to be more than a pair of perfect biceps," I tease.

He gives a wry smile. "And you're proving to be more than a perfect pair of—"

I spike a finger in the air. "Don't even think about it."

Bryson moves in close with a wicked grin sliding up his cheeks. He's more sex god than he is scholastic welcoming committee, and suddenly it feels as if he's navigating me to his chambers for a little coital inauguration. That tender place between my legs twitches with approval because if anyone is going to give me a little coital inauguration, I'd prefer it was him.

I try to ignore his oozing sexuality and let the mountain air distract me. The thick scent of pines perfume the vicinity with the slight after bite of fresh mountain soil. It's so pretty here with the tall emerald evergreens, the Sugar Maples with their leaves as wide as hands waving in the breeze. That's what I should be focusing on, the beauty in nature and not the ode to testosterone next to me who happens to be eliciting an electrical spark in the most intimate part of me with every third step.

We hit the crosswalk just as the light changes and cross the street with an entire herd of people. I'm not used to this mass of humanity. The entire population of the small town I'm from could fit right here in this crowd. A group of girls dressed in short skirts pass us. Their heads turn to check out Bryson, and the lean mean, machine he possesses as his body. The one with long black hair strokes his cheek as we walk on by.

"Looks like all the girls here are pretty friendly," I muse as we head toward a well-landscaped courtyard with a gilded sign reading, *Briggs Apartments, vacancies available! Inquire within.*

"Not as friendly as you, sugar." He gives a quick wink, and my stomach ignites like a burning coal. "Your roommate looked pretty friendly." He holds the door open for me, as we move into the overly air-conditioned building.

"Something tells me you'll find out for yourself exactly how friendly she is."

We step into the elevator and glide on up. Bryson inspects me from head to toe as if he were mapping me out with those spotlight eyes of his. It's like being under the scrutiny of a microscope each time he glances my way. It's as if he's looking straight into my soul, examining the flaws in the fiber of my being while reading my personal history like a textbook. Not that there's anything of interest to read. My life in general has been boring as toast. That seems to be the only consistency in my world.

God, I hope he's not some freak with a duffle bag fixation getting ready to chain me to his bedpost in some sadomasochistic lair. And the way that sultry smile keeps blinking on and off, I'm not too sure I'd mind. He's a bad boy, I can tell. I can spot them a mile away. I've got some serious troublemaker radar, and usually my gut warns me to steer clear, but there's something about this one that makes me want to fall to my knees and give him ten thousand lashes with my tongue in places that neither lashes nor tongues should ever venture. He's the exact type of guy Cole is forever telling me to stay away from. The kind that want nothing more than to nail me to the mattress, then forget my name by morning.

"Jeanie Waters." He nods, and I stare into him blankly because, holy shit, he's already forgotten my name. "That's your roommate," he continues. "And, for the record, I've already tapped that well."

I blink back with surprise. "Um, thanks for the info, I think? And *eww*. I honestly gave you a little more credit than that. I wouldn't have pegged you for a Greek who reduces women to water bearing vessels."

"Well you pegged me wrong—*twice*. For one, I'm not a Greek." We get off on the seventh floor, and he leads us to the nearest door. "And two, I'm not into degrading women to water bearing vessels, either." He slips a key into the lock, and the door opens to a clean looking living room with a pair of brown leather sofas, a TV the size of the wall. "I prefer notches."

"Very funny." I step in hesitantly. "So, you've lured me to your lair. Good trick. Is this where I get to test my rape whistle? Or do you prefer mace? I've got both handy." I pat down my jeans to confirm this theory and come up empty. Double crap.

"Lured you to my lair?" He moans it out as if trying to seduce me. "And here I thought you wanted to catch up on good times with your big bro?" He strides over to the hall and gives a psychotically loud knock over the nearest door. "Wake the hell up. You've got a visitor," he shouts.

"Tell her I don't want any." A muffled groan escapes from the other side, and I can peg that voice as Cole's any day of the week.

"He's still in bed this late in the afternoon? God, he must really be sick. I bet he's coming down with the flu or something." I touch my hand to my chest. "I'll see if I can get him some soup."

Bryson's chin dips a notch, and his eyes give me a smile all their own. "You might want to hold off on the fluids." He gives another set of walloping knocks over the door. "She says she's your sister," he shouts before setting his steel-colored eyes in my direction. A devilish grin rides low on his lips. He points to the door jam that divides the hall from the living room and skims his finger down a series of tally marks running in longitudinal lines. "Cole." He turns to the other side and points to an equally scratched surface. "Bryson."

"What's this?" I step over with caution in the event it's some frat boy trap that involves innovative ways to seduce braless freshmen.

"These, my friend, are *notches*." He leans in, and I can feel the heat emanating off his chest. His broad shoulders partially block the view of what looks to be my brother's name scribbled onto the wall.

"What are the notches for?" There's nothing but rows and rows of tally marks under my brother's name. "Is this some weight lifting game? Wait, let me guess, this

21

is somehow loosely related to wrestling." I roll my eyes at the thought. Cole has had an unnatural obsession with the sport since he was six.

"Wrestling?" His eyes hood over, and that lewd grin starts budding on his lips again. "You pegged it." He twists a smile that suggests otherwise.

A hard steady wallop shakes the walls, vibrating the tiny apartment.

"*God.*" I clutch at my chest as the banging continues. It's clearly coming from my brother's bedroom. "What the hell is he nailing to the wall?"

"Who." He bleats it out, doing his best impression of an owl—a hotter than hell, amazingly muscular owl, but nonetheless.

"Who what?"

"*Who* the hell is he nailing to the wall."

It takes a minute for what he's implying to sink in while the loud gunshot-like noises come to a crescendo and the distinct sound of deep guttural groans takes its place.

Everything in me seizes.

"You mean?" I point to the wall and door simultaneously.

"Exactly." He smears a satisfied grin. Clearly he's enjoying my newfound horror.

"Oh no." I take a few steps back to create some metric distance between myself and the perverted scoreboard. It's like I've fallen in some bizarre sexual wonderland, and for a minute I wonder if the plane went down, and I'm lying in a cornfield somewhere just barely clinging to life. "I'm sorry. I'm afraid you have the wrong Cole. Obviously some man-whore shares my brother's name. And, in no way do I want to stand in the way of his daily drilling. *My* Cole would never carve notches into his wall and have a serious headboard banging session in the middle of the afternoon."

"Oh really." He flat lines.

"Yes, *really*."

Bryson with the Biceps probably didn't hear me when I said *Brighton,* he was too busy pooling blood to the lower half of his body in hopes the rest of my clothes would spontaneously fall off. No wonder he's been following me around like a lovesick puppy. I've given him one serious boner to contend with, and now I can practically see the tally marks spinning in his eyes.

"Cole *Brighton*?" He nods, affirming my worst nightmare.

"Cole Brighton..." I stride back to the tally marks and inspect the sloppy row of lines crossed in groups of five that string all the way down the door jam. "Oh God, oh God, oh *God*." I spin, taking in the other side of the wall marked Bryson and inspect the hieroglyphics that predict his potential for a serious VD outbreak. And, judging by the magnificent scrawl, I'd say the odds of his dick falling off in the very near future are most definitely in his favor.

"This can't be right," I say, turning again in disbelief to inspect the sexual carnage my brother's engaged in since he's been away at Debauchery U. And, here, Mom and I thought he was buried in textbooks, losing himself in the stacks at the library. It looks like the only thing Cole has been burying himself in is an entire sea of vaginas. "Are there that many girls in North Carolina, or are you importing them in from out of state?" I bite down over my lip. Honestly, I don't know whether to laugh or cry. This has got to be a joke. "Me thinks these walls exaggerate just a tiny bit." Correction—a whole hell of a lot especially where my brother is concerned—at least they'd better.

Bryson lets out a laugh, and his sharpened canines flash, his teeth are white as milk. He's got that vampire, werewolf appeal to him, and my thighs quiver because I just so happen to have a sweet spot for all things vampire and werewolf right between my legs. Not that my sweet spot has ever entertained a beast of the paranormal variety, or human for that matter, but I digress.

"If anything I've been conservative with the effort." He leans in just above me, pinning me against the wall with his chest. His face inches in toward mine, and my stomach melts in a puddle of heat. "Your brother, however, has been known to be liberal with his chicken scratch." Bryson comes in closer and rakes his hot breath over my cheek. His perfect features inspire my heart to try and break free from my chest with its wild palpitations. My adrenaline spikes, and a bite of perspiration breaks out under my arms. I've never been so brazenly propositioned for a kiss, but knowing The Sultan of the Scoreboard, I think the offer extends to far more delicate places—like the aforementioned sweet spot.

The door explodes open, and Cole springs out with his dark hair rumpled, his glowing green eyes, twins to mine, and he looks startled by my presence.

"Baya?" He pulls me into a sweaty hug. "I wasn't expecting you until tomorrow." He's grinning ear-to-ear still holding me in a semi-headlock. His body smells ripe, and he's sticky to the touch.

"Mom managed to get me on an earlier flight." I give an impish grin as I make my way out of his strangle hold. "So, here I am. Surprise." I hold out my hands. It's only then I notice he's wearing nothing but boxers. Truthfully, this entire scenario has sort of turned the surprise around on me and not in any good way.

A brunette with a matted mane ambles out of his room and down the hall before shutting herself in what I presume to be the bathroom.

"Oh my God, it's true!" And I was the last person who was going to buy into the pornographic writing on the wall.

"What's true?" His dark brows furrow as he crosses his arms. Cole is gorgeous with those searing emerald eyes, dimples deep enough to sink your heart into. No wonder he's bedding his way through school. The girls aren't giving him a choice.

To my horror a beautiful blonde pokes her head out of his bedroom. She gives a slight wave at Bryson, and my stomach drops like a stone.

"You've got *two* in there?" My muscles seize. "You are not the Cole Brighton I grew up with. For sure you aren't the same Cole Brighton who called home once a week to lecture me on boys and their wandering penises." Because obviously he was speaking from experience.

"Penises?" Bryson mouths the word, and I choose to ignore him.

"What? We were having a study group." Cole frowns into me with a look that suggests I'd better believe him and quick.

He presses his hand over my back and ushers us to the couch.

"Study group, my ass," I whisper. And here I thought he was nothing like the playboys he preached long and hard for me to avoid, when all along he's been their fearless leader. Or should I say co-leader. I glare over at Bryson who's making himself comfy on a barstool nearby. He leans over the kitchen counter just gawking at the two of us as if readying for the show, and I can't help stealing glances. It's not my fault. He's handsome in an abnormal freak of nature kind of way, and his biceps seem to be taking my mind off the fact my sweet big bro was nothing but a big fat lie.

"So what's up?" Cole gives his signature dimpled grin. "Are you all settled in your dorm?"

"Yes." I shoot a quick look to Bryson and his prying eyes. "I *am*." I'm in no mood to run down the sins of my faux sister when my own flesh and blood has some serious carnal issues I'd like to contend with.

"Good." He runs his fingers through his thick black hair, totally unmoved by the fact he's in nothing but his skivvies. But, now that I've been made aware of the public service he's been generously gifting the ladies of Whitney Briggs, I'm sure it's far more clothing than he's used to. Cole props his feet up on the coffee table which would have been a felony offense if our type A mother were here. Of course, she would have been wild-eyed and pissed long before now—what with two girls streaming from his bedroom, his sex life mapped out like the periodic table of elements for all to see. That alone would have killed her on the spot, and she would never have made it to this new feet-on-the-furniture version of my brother. "You like your roommate?"

"Jeanine Waters." I nod. "Real friendly girl."

A dark laugh sputters from him as he pumps a fist over at Bryson, his comrade in tally mark wielding arms.

"She's a cool chick." Cole reaches for the remote, and the enormous television blinks to life. "You'll like her once you get to know her, but steer clear of her social circle. She's a party animal if you know what I mean. I'll set you up with some nice girls who like to hang out and read in their spare time, like you. Rumor has it there's a book club over at Prescott. You'll fit right in."

I try not to glance at Bryson who's just taken an obnoxiously loud bite of an apple while my cheeks burn through a dozen shades of red. It's one thing to be a self-proclaimed book nerd, but to have Cole announce it like its some social disease that forces bookworms to be exiled in a building together is another.

I clear my throat. "That sounds great, but I was thinking about busting out of my shell a little this year. You know, maybe joining a sorority?" Not really, but, now that the whole roommate thing isn't quite panning out how I hoped, it doesn't seem like such a bad idea.

"Rush is in a couple weeks." Bryson lifts his apple as if he were toasting my efforts.

"No." Cole shakes his head emphatically. "No rushing." He glares over at Bryson for commending the idea. "Baya this is Bryson my bonehead of a roommate. Don't listen to a word he says. Bry—this is my baby sister, keep your hands, and stupid ideas, the hell away from her." He turns back to me. "Besides she's not into guys."

"*What?*" This is news to me. "I am, too." I'm quick to rectify my sexual standing to the nipple ogler in the next room.

"No, you're not." Cole flips the channel until it lands on some football game. "You're like thirteen." He gives a sideways grin. "Besides, you're just a baby. You're not allowed to like guys. You can like guys in books. How's that? I hear book boyfriends are all the rage."

Thirteen? *Book* boyfriends? I glance over to Bryson, and my face heats up like a Texas sidewalk. The only thing in a rage around here is me.

"Sounds perfectly boring," I say it mostly to myself.

"That's my goal." Cole flips the channels again before settling on a cage fight. "I'm here to make sure your stay at Whitney Briggs is perfectly boring—and more than slightly educational."

The small harem from his bedroom saunters across the living room, holding their maxi-dresses at the knees and waving like pageant queens as they take off.

"See you tonight at Delta." The blonde blows a quick kiss to Bryson, but he still has those ice-colored eyes locked over mine.

Looks like Cole has a different set of standards for me than he does for himself.

"Perfectly boring," I whisper.

I glance up at Bryson, and my thighs quiver. He's branding himself over my skin, my heart, and not one bit of me wants to stop him.

I have a feeling my stay at Whitney Briggs is going to be anything but boring.

Bryson

The night sky above Delta house glows a deep purple. For a second I think this is a night where magic can happen, where people catch a lust driven fever and want to fall in love for the hell of it because they're miles from home, so why the hell not?

Sometimes I think that could be me, then I remember who I am, and what I've done, and the darkness seeps back in, filling in the void where hope once stood. I remember who I am and how much hurt I've caused—then the rose-colored glasses fall right off. I don't deserve to hold anyone's heart again, not now, not ever.

Delta house is teeming with girls sporting fresh tans, long, golden limbs and tits displayed with the cutting edge technology in boulder holders to exalt them to the point of perfection.

"Dude." Cole swats me in the stomach. "I'm headed for the hot tub. I might bring a crew home tonight if I'm lucky. I'll send you a bed warmer." He snatches a beer off the table before heading out.

It's hard to believe Cole and his sister Baya come from the same state, let alone gene pool. Cole has had a perpetual hard-on since the day I met him three years ago, and Baya seems like a lost duck in a hyper-sexualized pond.

"Look who's here?" A pair of arms circle around my waist, followed by the scent of cloying perfume. I peel her off before turning around.

"Aubree." Just who I didn't want to see.

Aubree Vincent is the exact kind of trouble I'm not interested in tonight or any other night of the year. I'd like to think I have standards. Aubree was Steph's best friend, and just about anything to do with Steph is sacred. I shake her out of my mind. I can't go there tonight. There aren't enough girls or beer to self-medicate from that pain.

Aubree's brassy blonde hair is spun in tight ringlets. Her roots are coming in strong. She has a knack for wearing too much makeup and not enough of anything else. Aubree has made a pass at me every day of the week and twice on Sundays for as far back as I can remember. High school blinks through my mind, and I swat it away like a fly.

Aubree and I happen to share an internship. I witnessed her going off on some poor girl in our group for not getting her coffee right, and that sort of killed any future boners I might have pointed in her direction. Since I've been at Briggs, I haven't been too picky about who I land in bed with. Both my heart and my dick have turned hard as steel since I've entered these hallowed halls.

"You feel like stripping down and getting wet?" She licks her bright pink lips.

I crane my neck toward the back window where I spot Cole with a bevy of lonely beauties and shake my head.

31

"Hot tub looks filled to capacity. And, you know me"—I shrug—"I'm a stickler for that damn fire code." She came down on me last week for having more than ten executives in a cubicle while I showed them an ad our competitor launched that happened to go viral. She actually busted my balls over the fire code of all things, which I hope sounded just as ridiculous now that I've handed the bizarre malfeasance back to her.

"Who said anything about the hot tub?" She lowers her false lashes and pulls me in by the belt loop.

"Aren't you the little vixen tonight?" I step in and press my hand to the small of her back. Maybe I should nail her and get it over with. God knows she's all but fallen on her knees trying to land me horizontal these past few years. But a part of me doesn't want to cave. A part of me wants to believe I've got standards somewhere in this depraved mind of mine, and I draw the line at girls who give more blow jobs than a leaf blower.

"*Vixen?*" She bites over her bottom lip so hard I expect to see blood. "Oh, sugar, for you? I can be anything you want," she purrs low in my ear, and my stomach turns as if I just downed a bad burrito.

"I'll have that Snap Track file done before next week." Maybe if I talk shop, she'll run in the other direction.

"Oh, hon"—her eyes expand showing off a network of bulging red lines—"the last thing I want to do is talk business." Aubree is the internship coordinator over at Capwell Inc., the ad agency that's my ticket into the corporate world once I graduate. Her uncle owns it, so she gets special privileges like busting my balls whenever the hell she feels like it. "As your boss, I forbid you to mix business with pleasure." She tracks her hand over my shirt, and a trail of chills explode up my spine.

A gorgeous brunette with long, sleek locks darkens the doorway—Baya. She's got on a pair of sky-high heels that tie to her knees and shorts that amount to not much more than a glorified zipper. She's traded her friendly tube top for a sequin tank, and I most certainly approve of her sparkling bosom, but something in me says Cole won't.

"Look, I better go." I pluck Aubree's nine-inch nails out of my back, and she pops them right back in.

"I'm not letting you off the hook so easy, honey." She leans in and takes a bite out of my ear. "I'm a little hungry, and I'm liking the menu a whole damn lot."

"Lucky for you there's an entire buffet of beefcake right out that door." I spin her toward the back and ditch into the crowd before she can render me lobeless.

My heart picks up pace as I scan the doorway, but Baya's nowhere to be found. I was sort of looking forward to showing her around, not that there's much to see here other than the requisite amount of liquor and sorority girls. The truth is, a part of me wanted to take up the big brother torch and protect her from the douches running rampant in this place. Not that I'm feeling brotherly toward her, quite the opposite. Baya has a sweetness about her that I hadn't seen since—

My mind starts to drift to the dark cave of the past, and I cinch it before I get too sucked in. I know what today would have been. I hadn't thought about Steph in so long—and yet something in Baya's eyes this afternoon reminded me of her. There's something downhome and innocent about Baya, and it's a far cry from what I'm used to around here. I would have bet every shiny dime I own that the last person she was related to was Cole screw-them-by-the-dozen Brighton.

A group of girls hanging out on the fringe of the room catch my attention, and I spot Baya standing by the keg, looking every bit the wallflower. Her dark hair falls seductively over one eye, and I swear a dimple just lit up in her cheek at the sight of me, at least that's the story I'm feeding my ego right about now.

I head over and swoop a cold one off the counter for her.

"For you princess." I hold back a smile that's begging to let loose. My dick twitches at the sight of her, hopeful to get laid because we both know it's been weeks. After years of bedding my way around campus, the local girls have lost their luster—not that I plan on bedding Baya. Cole would have my balls on a spit if I entertained the idea.

"No thanks." She makes a face at the amber bottle. It's only then I notice I'm holding it out in front of my jeans like some phallic extension. "I don't really drink."

"Oh, that's right. You're thirteen." I cinch a smile at my adolescent dig. I like teasing Baya. Nipplegate broke the ice, so we can only go up from there.

"I'm nineteen," she corrects. "And I don't drink because it's a personal preference. Trust me, if I wanted the beer, I'd take it. I just so happen to hate the taste of alcohol." She shudders. "I hate everything about it."

"I suppose this is a lousy time to tell you I work at a bar." That my family owns a whole string of them, but I leave that part out.

Her lime green eyes float up to mine. Her lips curve a naughty smile as if she's having her way with me mentally, and my dick starts knocking for attention again. I broaden my chest, trying to deflect my hard-on from launching into an all out crisis with no relief in sight.

"I couldn't care less where you work, Tyson." She smirks while peering around me into the crowd.

Damn she's hot when she's annoyed.

My brows knit. "It's *Bryson*." I glance down at her hot pink toenails and can't help but think they look like candy. Those shoes definitely have my attention, but it's her smooth creamy thighs that are making my mouth water. "I actually own the bars." I don't technically own jack, except maybe by way of inheritance, and judging by the way my dad keeps hitting the gym, that day is a long way off. Not that I wouldn't want it to be. "My family owns them," I fess up. Something about her has a way of dragging the truth out of me faster than expected. I'm not sure I've ever showed a girl the scoreboard, let alone filled them in on what it means. Sure it's out there in the open, but no one's ever questioned its relevance, or accused it of being remotely related to weight training or wrestling.

Baya continues to watch the crowd behind me. I glance back. She's eyeing about twenty different people, and at least half of them are jersey-wearing jocks. "I'm headed over to one in about twenty minutes if you want to join me. You could make some quick cash if you want."

"One what?" She takes a step to the right and gives a little wink at some dude in a Whitney Briggs sweatshirt.

"A bar—we've got a full menu, so it's more of a restaurant." Why does this conversation suddenly feel one-sided? "You could waitress if you want. It's a good way to line your pockets."

Her eyes narrow in on mine. Her lips purse, and it's becoming obvious she's visibly pissed.

"Look. I appreciate the offer, I really do." She floats her glowing eyes to mine, and her lips curl in a gutting, sexy way that make my balls ache for her touch. "I'm sure deep down under that mass of muscles you're a nice guy, but I prefer my first time to be with someone who doesn't swim in the hooker pool."

First time?

I run my gaze over her in this new light. Baya is gorgeous and sweet. She brings new meaning to the word beautiful. Of course she's a virgin—hell at nineteen she's barely legal.

She whisks by me and heads over to a group of helmet heads that have their biceps permanently flexed as a testament to their roid addiction. The one in the sweatshirt wastes no time in cupping her ass and makes her jump three feet in the process. His buddy pulls her in, and a dark smile stretches across his face at the prospect of fresh meat.

I head over and wrap my arm around her shoulder.

"Here you are," I say, leading her right out the exit and into the fresh night air. "So, have you reconsidered the offer? Up for some impromptu waitressing?"

She glances back at the frat house with its wild catcalls and army of panty-hungry jocks.

Baya swallows hard. "I don't see why not."

ಬಿಂಜ

"The Black Bear Saloon," I tell her as we drive down the highway. "That's the closest one to campus, but we've got two other places about a half hour away in either direction—the Sky Lab, and the Ice Bar. The Ice Bar is literally lined with ice, so you'll want to bundle up for that one." It's my father's crowning glory. Sometimes I think he appreciates the bars more than his own family.

"Excellent." She pulls at a strand of hair and twirls it around her perfectly long finger. Baya knows how to tease me like a master, and I'm pretty sure she's not aware of it.

"So what was a nice girl like you doing at a sleaze bag of a party? Delta is notorious for its inglorious hookups. There's a new strand of herpes that's been traced back to that very room we were standing in." Shit. Should I have said that? From now on I think I'll keep all references to communicable diseases to a minimum—that minimum being none.

"I don't doubt it." She pulls her shoulders back and arches her neck as if she's trying to seduce me, but I can tell she's just naturally sexy as hell. And, right about now, I'm regretting ever knowing her overprotective brother. The last thing I need to be doing it setting my dick compass on his little sister, but I have a feeling it's too late. The destination's been set, and, now, I have to figure out how to reprogram my balls before it's too late.

She sighs, and I wonder what it would feel like to have her making that noise in my mouth.

"I wasn't really planning on going out tonight but Jeanie had another 'guest' and, oddly enough, neither one of them were too shy about entertaining each another. Can you believe that?"

I shake my head while choking the shit out of the steering wheel because her cleavage just jumped as we took that last turn, and my semi-hard-on just graduated to the next phase in my Levis.

"It's like I'm invisible or something," she continues, and badly I want to interrupt and let her know my dick and I can attest to the fact she's very much visible. "One second I was organizing my books, and, the next, some guy drops his boxers and bends her over the mattress." She squeezes her eyes shut tight, and I steal a moment to envision Baya bent over my mattress. "I'm lucky I got out of the way in time."

A soft chuckle pulses through me.

"It's not funny." She swats me in the stomach, and a part of me wants to encourage a full on beating. "And, to make it worse, I'd swear on my dog's life, it was a different guy. What's wrong with you people here, anyway?"

"Wrong?" I consider this for a moment. There does seem to be a lot of random fornicating. She might be onto something. I shake my head as I pull into the lot of the Black Bear Saloon. It's the campus crawl, so I'd warn her to expect more of the same, but I'd venture to guess she's already caught onto the idea. "So, what kind of dog do you have?" I kill the engine and nod for her to hop out of the truck.

"Black lab," she says, as I meet up with her on the other side.

"Really? That's what I've got—well, my mom. My dad got the bars in the divorce—my mom got the house and the dog." Technically Dad bought Mom out, and, at the time, there was only one bar. What little she had left after paying her attorney went toward my sister Annie's education. She attends a private school for the deaf and hard of hearing. Dad pays out for her education too, but Mom's ego insists they split the bill, and, unfortunately for Mom, it hurts her bank account a little bit more.

Baya's eyes steady over mine, and, for a moment, I'm tempted to lean in and test out that luscious mouth of hers with a kiss.

"Yeah, well, I miss my dog like crazy." She bites over her cherry-stained lip. Baya glows against the backdrop of night like a lily. "Sounds like your mom got the better end of the deal."

"She did." I shake off a laugh. "Although she might deny it. She's trying to make ends meet as a realtor. My dad comes through every now and again, though." Great. Way to sound like I'm feeding her some financial bullshit about my family. The next thing I'll be telling her about is the time Holt stole my blankie when we were four and how I cried like a pussy for a week. "How about you? What do your parents do? I've been hanging out with your brother for almost half a decade, and I don't think he's mentioned them once."

"My mom does insurance billing for the local hospital, and my dad died when I was in eighth grade." She glances down at the concrete, and my heart drops to my feet.

"Sorry to hear that." Crap. I can't believe Cole's never mentioned it. "Can I ask what happened?"

She lets out a steady breath, and a layer of fog encircles her head like a frosted wreath. "He was a cyclist." The whites of her eyes glint in the moonlight, and I can tell she's tearing up. Way to bring up her misery. Looks like I'm up for the asshole of the year award. "One night, he went out for a ride, and he got hit."

"Shit," I whisper. "I'm sorry." I wrap my arm over her shoulders. "Look, if you'd rather do something else tonight I totally understand. It's your first night, and, if punching a time clock isn't you're idea of a good time, I get it."

"No, it's okay." She glances at the entrance with the overgrown bear looking ready to sexually assault the next patron and shudders. "Besides, I'm all for lining my pockets." She pinches at her barely-there shorts, and my dick weeps for her to touch it. "My clothes haven't quite arrived, so I may have raided Jeanie's closet without telling her." She twists her heels into the ground, and her cleavage bounces unexpectedly. "And shoes."

Baya sparkles under this dim light both inside and out. Her perfect lips are calling to me, red as rubies, hell, raspberries that I'd like to bite into. But she's not just some chick from Briggs I'm looking to bag, not some barfly ready and willing to drop in front of my Levi's, she's sweet—special—somebody's little sister. And if I keep saying it I might actually be able to defuse the bomb ticking in my boxers, but a part of me knows better. I'll be slicking one off in the shower later in her honor whether or not Cole approves.

I warm her arm with my hand and lead her up the walk.

"Let's go make some money," I sigh.

Deep down I know I have to have Baya. I need her to want me too, and I can't figure out why the hell I feel this way after knowing her for less than a few hours.

Baya Brighton has cast her spell whether she's aware of it or not, and, now, the only thing left to do is to figure out how the hell to break it.

I don't think I can.

I don't think I want to.

41

ജ൞

There's a trifecta of universities in the area that have turned the Black Bear into a hub of social civilization—although technically most nights are anything but civil. Having a central outlet like this has expanded the dating pool by three campuses and is half the reason there are so many damn tally marks on my wall to begin with.

Inside the bar, the mountain motif fits the area, unlike the upscale Sky Lab with its sci-fi feel or the Ice Bar with its literal frozen tundra. I can't wait to show Baya both of those places. What the hell am I saying? I glance down and give a polite smile, but my gut twists like a schoolboy at the sight of her. I need to stay the hell away from Baya, not drag her around to each of my family's establishments in hopes that a blowjob waits for me on the other end of the factory tour. I'm a moron for even looking at her. She's like crack, the more I'm near her, the more I need to have her.

"This is really nice." She looks around taking it all in, the mountain-themed tapestry lining the booths, the barstools carved out of gnarl wood. "So what do I do?"

"Start here." I pluck a small white apron from behind the counter and hand it to her. It's frilly and looks more like lingerie, but she doesn't seem to mind. Baya ties it low on her waist and with her micro-shorts it looks like that's all she's wearing.

Hot damn. I ride my gaze up her body, nice and slow, and my dick perks to attention.

"Who's this?" A woman's voice grumps from behind, and for a second I think I might find Aubree with her disgruntled lady boner, but it's not. It's Laney, one of the girls from school who works part time as a waitress. Her dark hair is pulled tight in a bun, and she's sporting her signature ultra-tight Black Bear T-shirt. Laney is hot in her own right, but she's not for me. Besides, she dated one of my good friends for a while last year. That sort of took her permanently off the roster.

"Laney." I pull her in. "This is Baya—Cole Brighton's little sister." Maybe if I keep reminding myself, out loud, many fucking times, that she's Cole's little sister my dick will back off.

Baya gives a disapproving smile in my direction before moving her glowing eyes to Laney.

"Cool name." She shakes her hand "And for the record"—she drags her eyes over to me again and shoots venom—"I don't care to be addressed as anybody's little sister. I'm just Baya." Her brows peak. For a moment she looks like she's about to invert my balls, but then she takes a breath and shows off every one of her perfect teeth with that killer smile. "Now teach me how to make some money."

"Food and soda only." I nod into Laney. The last thing I need is having our liquor license revoked within the hour.

Laney shuttles her off to the main floor as I make my way behind the counter.

"Well, look who decided to show?" Holt glances up from his martini shaker, and the gleam of stainless steel catches the light.

"Of course, I showed." I slap him on the back as I snap up a towel and wipe down the bar. "I wasn't about to let my big brother have all the *f-u-n*."

"Who's the hot chick? And why do I smell jail bait?"

"Relax, she's nineteen. And, yes, I told Laney she's only allowed to serve food and sodas. We're covered."

"Sweet." He frowns into her as she heads in our direction.

"This is great!" She beams, flaunting a bill in her hand before burying it in her pocket. "Some guy just gave me a twenty for wiggling my hips at him."

"*No.*" I shake my head. "No private dancing." Shit. Forget Cole, I'll have my own balls on a spit by the end of the night if she accidentally turns this into some kind of a stripping gig. The only one she's allowed to strip for is me. I give a dull smile because I know the only way I'll let that happen is in my fantasies, and I happen to have a couple lining up in the queue.

She wrinkles her nose and looks cute as hell in the process. "Okay, but the tips would be outrageous if I did."

"You know what else would be outrageous? Your brother's temper. Speaking of brothers—Baya, this is my big bro Holt—Holt, Baya."

"Nice to meet you." She gives an impish grin, and my dick whimpers like a sad puppy to come out and play.

"Baya," Holt eases her name out like a song. "You should see me mix a dirty martini." He leans in like he's diving for a kiss, and I slice my hand through the narrow gap between them.

"And, much like your big brother, mine is mostly full of himself."

She gives a quiet laugh. Her eyes sparkle like cut emeralds, and my heart races like it expects something from the exchange.

"On second thought"—I revert my attention back to Holt before I lose it looking at her—"he's more like an annoying little brother."

"*Hey.*" Holt taps his chest. "I'm older by fifteen minutes, and, much like tonight, your boyfriend here was late on arrival."

Her cheeks darken a shade at the thought of being called my anything. She probably considers it an insult, and who could blame her? It would be.

"So you're twins?" She tilts into me, and the tiny dimple in her cheek inverts.

"Fraternal," I say. "Or as I like to refer to him, the ultimate tagalong."

"Technically"—Holt wags a finger—"I came first, so you would be the tagalong."

"I *existed* first, instinctually I know this." I toss the dishtowel over my shoulder. "I'm also the smarter one, so don't believe half the bull he slings your way."

"Got it. Well, you look almost identical." She offers him a sly smile, and for a second I think she's flirting with him. "I'd better go." Her eyes linger over his before making her way back to the floor.

"Dude." I smack him in the arm until he comes to. "Don't even think of laying your paws on her."

"Sounds like someone's desperate to get laid." He folds his arms across his chest. "Wouldn't it be funny if this is the one that finally turns you down?"

I look over at her smiling at the customers, laughing while she takes their order.

"I don't have to worry about her turning me down. We won't be heading on that path." At least not anytime soon.

I don't deserve someone like Baya.

Steph can attest to that.

2

Take my Breath Away

Baya

Two weeks crawl by, and I've yet to officially "meet" my roommate.

Jeanie Waters is an enigma, or an enema, take your pick. But, perhaps more to the point, she's a budding porn star. I've seen more female anatomy the last fourteen days than I have in a lifetime of showers and baths. I swear I could work as a police sketch artist, detailing out vulvas and penises in microscopic detail when necessary.

Silly me. I always thought my first glance at the male anatomy would have some stamp of romance to it, and I guess if you count the fleshy offensive Jeanie partakes in as "romantic" then I would have been right.

I wake to the sound of grunting and dread to open my eyes. I give a groggy glance over in her direction only to find her overgrown pink nipples bouncing at a dizzying pace. I withhold the urge to wave at Thing One and Thing Two. Sadly, they're more friendly with me than she is. The polite girl in me wants to say good morning to the twins, but I resist the urge.

I groan as I swing my legs out of bed.

"Sheesh. Don't you ever take a break?" I slip into my flip-flops as some dark-haired boy smiles from behind her. *Gah!* He's waving and penetrating, and I'm fifty shades of creeped out. "That's it," I hiss, throwing crap into my Whitney Briggs duffle bag at random. My luggage finally managed to arrive, but this time I'm only taking the basics. I doubt Jeanie or her steady line of boy-toys will bother to pilfer through my father's extensive collection of Hardy Boys novels, so I'll pick those up later. It's Friday, and I don't have any classes, but, unlike the rest of the student population, I won't be soaking in the Z's until late afternoon, I'll be hitting the road, homeless for the rest of the semester. It takes less than five minutes to clear most of my crap and snap up my backpack before hightailing it out of there.

I don't bother waiting for the elevator. Instead, I bolt down the stairwell and head straight for the outdoors. The weather has already turned for the worst since the day I arrived. The air is crisp as an apple, and there's a bite of fall all around us even though technically it's the tail end of summer. Back in Texas the ground is still baking, *sizzling* under my mother's feet, but here it's cool as an iceberg, and you can take in large lungfuls of air without choking on the desert dust.

The Briggs Apartment building comes up on me quick, and before I know it I'm riding the elevator up. Bryson let me work alongside him at the Black Bear last weekend, and I'm sort of hoping he'll rekindle the offer tonight. I'm more interested in Bryson than I am in brushing up on my waitressing skills, but I made over two hundred bucks last Friday and Saturday combined, so I'm not complaining about the income boost either. Technically it's not a boost since anything is more than nothing.

I give a gentle knock over their door and wait a moment. It's still pretty early, so I doubt either one of them is awake. I turn the knob, and, sure enough, it's unlocked, so I let myself in and land my stuff behind the couch. Back at my place, the OCD in me makes sure I check that the door is bolted shut at least twelve times before I go to bed, and, here Cole and Bryson all but leave an invitation for the ax murderers in the neighborhood. On second thought, my brother probably has an open door policy with the surrounding sororities. He's probably blanketed the neighborhood with flyers that read, *Need an orgasm to take the edge off that next exam? Head to Cole's! Bring a friend to double your pleasure. Summa cum loud. Summa cum quiet. Come one, come all!* What a moron my brother is turning out to be.

I head over to the wall of shame and start counting tally marks, the one's on Bryson's wall first. I'm halfway through the first row when a soft click emits from the hall, and a pretty blonde with a skintight tank top ambles out of the back bedroom. Her rear is hanging out, and I force my eyes to pop back up to hers in the event I'm tempted to see if the carpet matches the drapes.

"Hi," I say it stunned, suddenly regretting ever coming because I know for a fact the last time I checked that wasn't Cole's bedroom. It's Bryson's. Just the thought has my heart turning to stone and crashing to my feet.

She combs her bangs with her fingers and heads to the bathroom as if I wasn't even visible. *God*—she probably thinks I'm standing in line.

The door opens again, and this time it's a very disheveled looking Bryson Edwards, and, for sure, now I wish I was invisible.

Oh God. Take me now.

His head dips back a notch, and he looks around as if to confirm the fact he's not hallucinating. "You just hanging out?"

"Um...yeah." I bite over my bottom lip because suddenly I feel ridiculous counting tally marks while he's busy making them. I don't know why in the hell it would bother me to see a pretty blonde slink out of his bedroom. I don't know why in the hell I couldn't stop thinking about him for the last two weeks—except maybe those washboard abs have something to do with it, or those pale eyes, or that blessed-by-God face...

I run my tongue over my lips while staring down at his chest like I'm about to eat an entire stack of pancakes off it, and a part of me wishes I were. His boxers are pulled so low I can see the perfect V leading to his—

"My roommate was at it again." I shake my head, trying to snap out of the trance his boy parts have unwittingly pulled me into. "I can't shut her off—

personally I think she's some high tech sex toy." My insides tingle just looking at him, and now I wish I had a high tech sex toy to take the edge off. The Bryson 2000 model to be exact. And if that bulge in his boxers is telling the truth, it's the extra-large version, for sure.

The blonde skank saunters back into the hall before I can finish my thought. God. I wish the carpet would open up and swallow me whole. Or maybe they have one of those Venus flytraps lying around, so I can go and curl up between its meat-eating leaves. I've never once *not* wanted to be somewhere this bad, save for my father's funeral.

"Look, I can go—I *should* go." I turn to grab my things, but his arm lands heavy and full around my waist preventing me from taking a single step. Everything in me sighs at his warm, strong touch. My lids flutter as a strong surge pulsates deep inside me, and I swear I've just had one of those G-spot mythological orgasms that half the women on the planet think are fiction spun by men to make women feel sexually inadequate.

"Stay," he presses his searing abs against my back, and his voice vibrates down my neck, heated and sultry. "I want you to." He smells like sex, and his skin is moist with perspiration, and I should be twelve kinds of disgusted right now, but I'm not. A quiver ripples through my stomach, and it takes a moment for me to catch my breath. Bryson Edwards is holding me in a quasi-embrace, and I never want him to let go.

"I'd better make tracks." The blonde leans in and kisses him on the cheek, awkwardly sandwiching me between them. God, she's probably *used* to sandwiching other girls between them. Maybe that's how Bryson and my brother have managed to amass so many tally marks in the first place—*threesomes*. I shudder at the thought. Although, right about now, I wouldn't take the idea off the table if it entailed Bryson and his strong hands dispelling a thousand myths that surround the female anatomy.

"I've got roll call in ten minutes." She pulls back and frowns into her phone. Her face is tanned to perfection, she's got bee-stung lips to die for, and her cleavage miraculously balloons the way God intended. Well, maybe not God—more like Victoria's Secret, but, nevertheless, the premise is the same. There's no way in hell I can ever compete with that. "So are you new?" She blinks her dark eyes at me, and honest to God, outside of Laney, this is the only other female that's acknowledged my presence these past two weeks.

"Freshman." I'm not in the mood to have a faux conversation with the girl who just slept with my imaginary boyfriend, besides—his strong arm is still wrapped warm around my waist, and now I've got multiple orgasms to contend with. Wait. Is that what he is? My imaginary boyfriend? Shit. This is getting serious.

"Cool!" She hops on her toes as if freshman, in and of themselves, were an anomaly. "Meet me in the quad at noon, better yet, what's your name?"

"Baya Brighton." I have a feeling I'll be regretting this seemingly innocent exchange.

"Perfect." She jots it into her phone. "Consider yourself rushing for Alpha Chi. Now Aubree won't give me shit for being late." She presses another kiss into Bryson's cheek and inadvertently crushes me against his rock hard body. "I've already met my recruiting quota for the day. See you Monday at four, Alpha Chi—don't be late!" She waves and bites the air at Bryson before slamming her way out of the apartment.

Cole's doorknob rattles, and Bryson lets go of me and takes a full step back. Cole swings his door open, good and pissed.

"Dude," he groans into Bryson, looking equally sexually disheveled. "Baya?" His eyes bulge as he takes me in. "What the hell? Did you touch my sister?" He charges at Bryson with his chest pulled back like a gorilla.

"No!" I'm quick to step between them and avert a physical altercation. "*No*, he didn't." But all of my girl parts wish to God he did.

I place a hand on either of their chests as if to keep them apart, but really I'm taking a moment to molest the hell out of Bryson's abs—and, just as I suspected, he's carved from oven-heated marble. "I was just about to crash on the couch"—I hesitate for a second, dripping my fingers down Bryson's chest—"like all weekend." I try to bat my lashes at him in an ill attempt to flirt, but he's got my stomach knotted up in a bundle of nerves, and I want to cry because it feels like I'm invisible to him as well.

"Anyway, I sort of need to catch up on some serious beauty sleep."

"No, no, no...." Cole groans into the idea.

"Yes, yes, yes," I counter. "*He* said it was okay." I smile over at Bryson with the lie still fresh on my lips. At least I'd like to think he'd say it was okay if I had asked— offered up his bedroom maybe...his *body* to keep me warm.

"That's right." Bryson gives an apprehensive nod. His glacial blue eyes pulsate over mine as if speaking in code. There's an undeniable pull taking place. Bryson has power over me whether I like it or not. "I'm just going to jump in the shower real quick. Either of you guys want to hit breakfast in a little while?"

"*Cole.*" A girl's voice emanates from deep in my brother's bedroom. Seriously? Does anybody sleep alone around here?

"Nah, I've got more important things to do." Cole glances over his shoulder.

More important things, or *people* to do? I want to ask but don't. Just thinking about what goes on in that love shack of his makes my stomach turn. Come to think of it, this entire place is probably heavily coated with genetic forensics I want no part of, especially the couch.

Cole socks Bryson in the arm. "Why don't you guys go ahead."

"Will do." Bryson glances over at me with the ghost of a smile before disappearing down the hall.

Cole wags his finger at me to come in close.

"What?" I openly glare into the dark pit behind him. "By the way, Mom is going have an aneurism when I tell her what a testosterone-laden beast you've morphed into."

"Baya." He closes his eyes a moment. "Please don't say a word to Mom." He digs his fingers into his eyes in an effort to wipe away his sleep. "Anyway, I thought I heard something about rush." Cole shakes his head without verbalizing his disapproval. "Trust me, Alpha Chi is the last place you want to be."

"Sounds like some backward cheer." I'm only half-teasing because I can feel my blood boiling just beneath the surface. "This isn't going to turn into another book club lecture is it? Because in case you haven't noticed—and you probably haven't because you're too busy jonesing for condoms—I'm in college now, and I plan on having a life for once." Life is code for fun which just might be code for penis, but I'm not brave enough to admit it.

"Hey"—his eyes soften into mine, and for the first time since I've arrived it's like looking in a mirror—"I want you to have a life. I really do. It's just I don't want you mixed up with the wrong crowd. I want you to have a *good* life."

"Cole," the girl's voice hums from his bedroom.

"Sounds like you're living the good life," I muse. I don't really care for the double standard he's imposing. I'd call him out on it, but I'd rather not toss around the word *hypocrite* before seven in the morning.

"Just do us both a favor and don't rush. Trust me, the last thing you want to be is a 'sorority' girl." He says *sorority* like it's a new strain of herpes.

"*Excuse* me!" The girl laughs while nailing him in the back of the head with a pillow. I smell a Greek tragedy in the making.

"I'd better let you go." I glance into his room before looking him right in the eye. "Looks like things are about to get violent. Be careful in there." I don't bother wavering from my hard stare. Cole has systematically been pushing all my buttons by pulling the big brother card every time I turn around. I'd hate to break it to him, but the more he tries to push me into the arms of a fictional boyfriend, the more I'm tempted to add my name to the wall of horrors and start chalking up my own damn tally marks. And if he tries lecturing me on the benefits of being a good girl one more time, I swear I'll put every penis on notice well before afternoon. But he doesn't.

I head over to the couch and hear the door to his room click shut, the sound of incessant laughter on the other side, then a slam and a whack. Something tells me a little more than a pillow fight just broke out.

ഇൗരു

"Sorry." I apologize to Bryson for the tenth time as we head outside of the building. "It's just, my roommate is making me *insane*. Honest to God, I'm looking forward to her menstrual cycle just so the both of us can finally get some rest."

He huffs out a laugh, and I'm entranced with the way the slight impression of a comma slices up his cheek.

"Sorry—TMI, I know." I shake my head. "But I haven't been able to get one ounce of studying done in that room." Mostly it's Bryson's fault because I can't stop thinking about him. He's become my singular obsession like no other boy has, and, now, I'm going to have breakfast with his mouthwatering abs.

"You don't need to apologize—especially when you've done absolutely nothing wrong. Jeanie's the one who should say she's sorry."

I glance down at my lavender flip-flops, my questionable level of dress, considering I'm wearing the tiny cotton shorts I slept in and a WB sweatshirt.

Maybe I shouldn't care that Jeanie Waters is having marathon sex. Maybe I should be running from Cole's apartment because of the very same reason. Listening to Cole satisfy his jock itch is just as bad.

"Sometimes I wonder if coming here was nothing but a big mistake."

"Hey." He wraps his arm around my shoulders, and my entire body demands to mold to his, so I do. "I'm glad you're here." Bryson smells like soap, mountain fresh with a hint of mint. I glance up at him as his eyes pull along my features slowly with a strangled angst that I can't quite categorize. "Laney was pretty darn glad you were here last week to help out, too. Speaking of which, are you up for catching some hours tonight? I'm working at the Sky Bar. Same drill, less skill." He twists his lips, and my stomach pinches with heat. God knows I don't have any skills when it comes to the opposite gender, but I'd love for him to teach me.

"*Yes.*" I practically accost him in the process by wrapping my arms around him tight. "I mean"—I take a step back, trying to play it cool—"that's totally fine."

"Great. Now let's get to the task of nourishing you so you can last until three in the morning." His arm slinks down to my waist and leaves a line of fire in its wake. "Oh"—he puts his hands in the air like a thief—"sorry."

A bus hisses down the street, and my hair flies up like a thousand little snakes from the gust of wind, but I can't break my gaze from Bryson and those gorgeous pebble blue eyes. A smile tugs at his lips, but he won't give it and my heart wrenches.

"I'm not sorry," it comes out barely a whisper. I'm sure he didn't hear, but a part of me wishes he did—that he wasn't sorry either.

"You want to go for a ride?" He motions to the sea of bicycles tethered to the front of the building. "I mean, I know you mentioned your dad rode, and I totally get it if you don't want to, I just thought—" Bryson lets his words hang in the air. He runs his tongue over his lips, quick as lightning, as if he didn't know what else to do with himself. My arms beg to fit themselves around his body. He's watching me again in that deep knowable way that suggests he's peeling back my skin to see what's really underneath, and my face burns with heat.

"I'd love to go for a ride. In fact, that's exactly what I'm saving my tips for—a shiny new bike." My throat goes dry, so I clear it. "Well, maybe not so shiny since it'll most likely come from the nearest thrift shop, but it'll be new to me."

"You may not have to save as much as you think." He breaks out in a slow-spreading grin and leads me over to a pair of bikes, before unleashing them both from their chains.

"Why do I get the feeling I'm going to have all of Alphi Chi after me for bike theft?"

"You won't." He tweaks his brows like he's flirting, and my insides do a cartwheel. "It's your brother's. He hardly uses it. He prefers his penny board when it comes to cruising campus. Besides, if he reports it missing, you won't do much time behind bars—three, four months tops."

"*Nice.*" I smack him over the shoulder. "Bike theft, huh? I had a feeling you were a bad boy." My eyes widen as he pauses to look at me, and for a second I think I've crossed some invisible line.

"I am a bad boy." He hops on his bike, and I do the same. "That's exactly why you should stay far, far away from me." His chin dips, his eyes cloud over like maybe he means it.

"Be quiet and feed me." I laugh as he leads the way.

80C3

We peddle out past the university, past the row of Greek mansions with their boxy chic exteriors, their well-manicured lawns, and over to a rundown strip mall that's badly in need of a paint job.

Bryson points over to a donut shop, and I give an eager nod because everyone knows that donuts and coffee are the breakfast of champions.

"You mind if I run in and grab it to go?" He gives a sheepish smile as he climbs off his bike. "There's someplace I'd like to take you."

"Not at all." My heart thumps at the thought of where this mysterious place might be. And by "take you" I'm hoping he means sexually. Bryson has girls for breakfast lunch, and dinner, I don't see why I should be off the menu. If those tally marks attest to anything it's that his penis isn't all that picky.

"Any requests?"

"Chocolate," I shout as he starts to head in. "Oh— and throw in a jelly filled!" I should have said cream filled and got his wheels turning.

A rise of heat filters through me as I give a casual nod, but everything about this feels anything but casual. God—it actually feels like a *date*. I should write Jeanie a thank you note—or, more specifically, her insatiable vagina, although I doubt either of them would know who sent it.

Bryson reappears in record time, and I follow him out as a soft haze fills the streets.

A sign appears that reads, *Welcome to Hollow Brook* as the city turns decidedly rural, and strip malls are replaced with dense emerald pines. The air cools as we ride to higher elevations. My thighs called it quits about ten minutes ago, but my lips won't let the protest fly as I soldier on right behind Bryson.

He pulls us off onto a dirt path, and we head into a clearing that opens to a cloud of vapors emitting from a tiny pool of water. It's partially hidden behind a series of boulders, and it looks like a dream, a fairytale.

"What is this place?" I try to not to sound so out of breath as I park my bike alongside his. My legs feel like rubber as I walk over to admire the view. If Bryson *did* want to have his way with me, I might collapse and lay there like a corpse. Not exactly the way I envisioned losing my virginity.

"The Witch's Cauldron."

We take a seat on the lowest boulder overlooking the aquamarine spring, the perfect size of a hot tub, and Bryson pulls me in by the waist. My breathing ceases. Dear God, he *did* drag me out into the middle of nowhere just so he could have his way with me!

"Wow"—I clear my throat—"it's so amazingly beautiful." I gaze into the tiny pool as a layer of mist wafts over the surface.

"It is beautiful." His hand grazes mine as he passes me a cup of coffee, and my entire body breaks out in a fit of perspiration. "So are you."

I suck in a quick breath and hold it. I've never had that kind of a compliment before, certainly not from a sex god like Bryson. Although, he did already add a tally mark to his wall this morning. Maybe he's going for double or nothing? With my luck he's still on autopilot, and the compliments are just a part of the carnal package.

"Thank you." I take a sip of coffee only to burn the tip of my tongue. "You don't have to practice your pick up lines around me." I land my hand over his arm to push him off but don't have the will to do it. "I'm not really in your league." I glance down at the rim of my coffee, embarrassed by my admission, true as it might be.

Honestly? Could I have let fifteen minutes go by without dragging us into the awkward zone?

"I don't have a league." His eyes meet with mine before he removes his arm and opens the tiny pink donut box with half a dozen sugared treats staring back at us. "But if I did, I'm pretty sure I'd let you in." He pushes into me playfully with his shoulder, and my body lights up with hope.

I glance up at him and hold his gaze, heavy as steel. "According to those tally marks, you let a lot of girls in."

"Touché."

"Jelly." I hold up a donut. I'd better shove it into my mouth before anymore word-vomit oozes out of me. The next thing I'll be telling him is that I want to pull a Jeanie

Waters with him and commence the fuck-fest immediately. That pool of steaming water looks like a good place to start, although I'm betting he's already "tapped that well," too. I bet there's nowhere he hasn't committed a carnal crime and not very many girls he hasn't committed them with. Except, of course, me, and now it's quickly becoming evident I'm on a mission to rectify that.

"So tell me about your classes." He's not eating. He's not even holding his coffee. He's simply observing me as if he really cared to know.

"U.S. History is going to be a bear. The professor hates me, I can tell." I sweep my gaze over his chest and am startled to see how close he's sitting. I could have sworn you could have parked a bicycle between us a moment ago. "And, I already have three papers due in a two week span between that and lit. It looks like I'll have to pull a few all-nighters—but secretly I've been looking forward to those." I push into his shoulder like he did mine, and my arm lights up with heat from the exchange. "I'm a nerd that way."

"I'm a nerd that way, too." He pushes back, and, for moment, I think our little donut exchange might parlay into an all-out wrestling match, jelly and all. "You do realize Jeanie has a few all-nighters planned herself. I doubt you'll get much done at your place." He bites into a glazed donut, and half of it disappears.

"For sure I won't, but I could probably get some great footage and make millions off a sex tape. 'Jeanie does Whitney Briggs.' Who needs this whole edjumacation thing anyway?" I try to rival his donut eating skills and fail miserably by smearing jelly up the side of my cheek. I'm quick to wipe it off, but with my luck it probably looks like a massacre just took place.

A grey dove darts from the bushes and soars into the sky, leaving a trail like pencil lead through the haze, but Bryson doesn't notice it. For whatever reason the only thing he seems to notice is me. He touches his finger to my cheek and swipes a small spot of jelly off then holds it in the air for me to see before licking it clean.

Holy shit.

"You should ditch that whole dorm thing and hang out with Cole and me." He pushes into my arm again, and this time he stays there with his shoulder butted up against mine, and, holy hell, my girls parts are feeling some damn good vibrations right about now. His thigh is so close to my leg, I can feel the warmth radiating from him like an inferno.

"I'm one step ahead of you." I swallow hard. "I've already got my bags packed. But don't worry. I won't cramp your style for long. I plan on scoring a room at Casa Alpha Chi. Did you see the size of those Greek houses?" As much as I'd like to talk about expensive looking real estate, I can't help but quiver from his touch. My entire body feels as though it's about to combust. One more touch and I'll embarrass myself by having an all-out screaming orgasm in front of him.

"I have seen those houses, and I've also had the pleasure to roam those halls. You'll be living it up in the lap of luxury once you're in."

"You think I'll get in?"

"Yes." His brows rise into his forehead. "They'd be insane not to want you."

My insides melt at the thought of him believing in me—wanting me.

"I haven't had this kind of encouragement since my dad died," I say it soft, unwarranted. "Not that my mom doesn't care, but she's been a little overly cautious with me since he passed away. In fact, Cole is the only reason she green-lighted Whitney Briggs to begin with. I guess she thought having my brother around would be the equivalent of body armor." A chastity belt is more to the point, but I don't dare share the imagery with Mr. Edwards. Besides, my girl parts are on the cusp of sending a personalized invite to his boy parts, and I'm not about to stop them.

"He sort of is." His eyes widen because we both know he's already been threatened to steer clear. Anyway, I'm sure a god like Bryson Edwards thinks of me as no more than a little sister, himself. Who am I kidding? Even *I* thought the girl that kissed him goodbye this morning was hotter than hell.

"So was that your girlfriend?" If I'm going to pull us into the awkward zone, I may as well commit.

A bird chirps, an entire array of strange animal sounds purr and hiss in the distance as Bryson tries to figure out exactly what the blonde bimbo from Alpha Chi could have meant to him.

"Jules is just a girl in a long string of girls."

I like the way he reduced her to the human equivalent of a paper chain. Something cheap you could throw away on a whim.

"*Notches*," I correct. A lizard saunters up the rock before spying us and quickly scurrying away.

"Yeah, well, I think I'm going to hang it up and hand the reins over to the king. I'm no match for your brother's testosterone superpowers. I think I'll yield to the master and let him take the throne. It *is* senior year. One of us was bound to be defeated."

"Really?" My heart thumps wild in my chest as a series of low lying clouds move in and steal the sunshine from the watery blue sky. "What's going to happen to your man parts?" My eyes widen, my cheeks blush bright as candy apples as if I had outright propositioned him. "I'm sure there are some serious ramifications to denying them their regularly-scheduled testosterone release. Rumor has it blue balls are a very real thing."

"I've taken a cold shower or two in my time." His steely gaze locks onto mine, and all of nature goes off like a siren around us. It's as if the birds, the bees, and every creature known to man is cheering us on, every living creature except for Bryson, of course. I'm pretty sure his vow of celibacy has very little to do with me—unless, of course, I nauseate him—kill his appetite for all things estrogen.

"Cold showers, huh?" I edge my face in toward his to see if he'll bite. Bryson glances down at my mouth and wets his lips. He's eyeing me like a snake that might jump out and inflict him with a venomous bite. I've kissed a few boys in my time, and leaning in like this was all the nudging it took, just a little movement in the right direction, and before I knew it, their tongues were being fed to me by the inch. But Bryson doesn't move. He doesn't breathe or say a word. He just stares me down as if a standoff at high noon were taking place—his testosterone against my estrogen. His eyes widen. His shoulders nudge toward mine, but he stops and presses his lips together as if he's made up his mind not to continue.

We finish our donuts, and he races me downhill all the way back to campus.

He lets me win, and I'm okay with that for now.

Bryson is the real prize.

I wonder if I can win his heart like he seems to be winning mine?

Bryson

Baya looks damn hot tonight in her barely-there jean shorts, her pink workout bra that annunciates two of her greatest assets. She's strutting her stuff at the Sky Lab, walking over the lunar-inspired flooring as if she owned the place. Lucky for her, one of the waitresses on duty had to go home early, and now she has twice the tables she had last week.

"This is fantastic." She waves a ten-dollar bill in my face. She's so damn beautiful, I can actually feel my balls weeping in her presence. "Those guys weren't even here five minutes after their food arrived. I keep scoring the big bills like this, and I might trade in U.S. History for my new—might I add lucrative career—as a waitress."

"I'd hang onto the books if I were you," I say, passing a group of shots off to the drink waitress. She doesn't looks so thrilled with the fact Baya is here, but I didn't take an opinion poll, so it really doesn't matter. "You can always wait tables once you're through with school, but you won't get these years back, and, who knows? You might regret not going." Holt runs through my mind. "My brother decided to chase his tail after high school and now laments the fact I'm getting ready to graduate. But, if you did quit, you could always go back. At least that's what I tell my brother." I give a sober nod. "He didn't bother showing up, and now wishes I kicked him in the balls until he did."

"You're pretty encouraging, you know that?" Her doe eyes blink up at me a smooth lime green, and I want to lose myself just staring in them. "Usually I hear the opposite from Cole and Mom. You know—do as you're told, not as you wish. Not that I want to quit school or anything. I just got here, and I really like it so far." Her face lights up pink as cotton candy, and I swallow hard at how fucking gorgeous she is—how preciously sweet. I wish she wasn't. I wish she was hell on heels, wearing the bitch suit of armor twenty-four seven—that she was just some girl in a sea of Whitney women. I might have done her by now if she was either of those things, but she's not. Baya has the face and body of an angel. She has me shaking every time she's around, and yet she's off limits. Not because of anything Cole said, but because I say so.

"I'm glad you're sticking around." I take a breath. I can tell by the way she's been looking at me all day she's feeling something. I should probably end this right now before things get too out of hand. Baya deserves someone as gentle as she is—someone who'll tell her he loves her and mean it before ever thinking about taking her to the bedroom. A part of me would die to be that person, but deep down I know I can't.

A barfly pops up at the counter—a plastic girl with a spray on tan, hair bleached of all its natural color, leaving a dry straw-like mess in its wake. That's who I should be pining for tonight. For sure I shouldn't be entertaining

Baya with her wonderstruck lust for me. I'm not the person she thinks I am. I'm not even close.

I head over to the blonde who's already trying to impress me and my dick by showing off the cherry stem she's tied in a knot with her tongue.

"It takes a talent." I lean in and smolder into her, letting her know with every nonverbal cue, she's about to get lucky tonight. I glance back at Baya and catch the viral look of grief sweeping across her face.

Crap. I can't do this.

"If you need something, just ask Jim." I call the backup from the other end of the bar and head over to Baya. "Now where were we?" I press out a sad smile. "Oh, that's right, we're both really glad you came."

The rest of the night Baya glows and shines as she swindles customers out of their hard-earned dough with nothing more than that million-dollar smile. I watch her tight little bottom in those barely-there shorts as if I were her personal security team. Each passing minute I try to picture what it would be like to hold her, to twirl my tongue in her ear just to hear her moan and giggle. I watch as her lips curve and imagine she were doing it for me while lying beneath me without any clothes on—how soft her perfect body might be.

The clock strikes three, and we do the world's fastest close before I whisk her into the cool night air.

The lamp from the parking lot illuminates her like an angel. The lot has cleared out, leaving just my truck for as far as the eye can see. It's just Baya and me. And no matter how hard I want to resist it, I like it like this, a whole hell of a lot.

"So what's the haul?" I nod into her overstuffed shorts.

"I think it's over a hundred, but I'm afraid half of it will blow away if I try to empty my pockets." She rubs her bare arms, and her teeth clatter like castanets.

"Here." I pull off my sweatshirt and glide it over her so fast, she can't protest.

"It's so *warm*." She yanks it down past her knees, and it springs back up to her bottom.

Baya looks up and gives a shy smile, her sweet perfume pulls me in, and I can't help but get caught up in the moment. It takes everything I've got not to bury my face in her hair, pull my lips over her neck. Earlier today she wanted a kiss. I've been to the rodeo enough to know what's about to go down, and she outright begged for one while we were on that boulder. Every part of me wanted to give it, but I held strong. I'm not feeling too strong right about now. My mouth wants to cover hers. My body wants nothing more than to wrap itself around her like a blanket.

She hedges in and folds her arms around my waist.

"Baya," I whisper with an unspoken agony I hope to never relive. It's coming—all those feelings I had so long ago. I swore I'd never go there again. I need to stave them off—deny them. It's the only way I know to keep my heart safe—hell, keep *Baya's* heart safe.

"Is something wrong? Is it me?" Her eyes round out in horror as if maybe I'm repulsed by her.

"No." My hands float up to her waist, and I brush over her hips with my fingers. Baya is soft, her hair smooth as silk. I lean in and inhale her scent while touching down over the top of her head with my cheek. God she smells nice—like vanilla and cinnamon and suddenly I'm very fucking hungry for vanilla and cinnamon. "You're perfect, I promise." A little too much.

"Is it Cole?" she whispers. She knows I'm stalling and demands to know why.

Cole is the easy out. I should take it and run with it all the way back to Whitney Briggs. A part of me wants to evict Jeanie from her dorm just to keep Baya a safe distance from me for the rest of the night—hell, the rest of the year. But I'm right there, I'm about to cave and when I do I'll take everything she's willing to give me.

"No, it's not Cole." I shake my head in defeat. The last thing I want to do is lie to her.

Tears well up in her eyes and she blinks them back. Crap. Now I'm humiliating her. That's the last thing on the planet I want to do.

"Bryson"—her voice breaks—"do you think maybe we could share just one kiss?" The desperation, the outright pleading in her voice kills me on a primal level and my body starts to shake because I want that kiss just as bad as she does. Probably more.

My adrenaline picks up until my heart feels like a bomb is about to detonate in my chest. What the hell. It's just a kiss. Although a part of me knows it will be anything but just a kiss with Baya.

I cradle her cheeks in the palms of my hands and draw her to me, slow and measured. I give a gentle smile as her eyes close, her lips part waiting for mine to greet her. I want to freeze this moment. This is innocent and pure—untainted from my past in a way that I wish the rest of my life could be.

"Baya," her name strains from my lips as threadbare as the wind as I bring my mouth to hers. I offer a barely-there pass, soft as down feathers before landing hard over her mouth like I want to, like I've wanted to ever since that afternoon she first arrived. I swipe my tongue over hers and a groan rips from my gut as if it's waited all my life to come out. A burst of passion releases from me like I have never known. I've waited years for a kiss just like this one—an entire lifetime. I had never had a kiss that mattered so much—that I've craved so badly before and now I know why—Baya wasn't there to give it.

Steph tries to surface but I hold down the past and refuse to let it cork to the top. This is my moment with Baya and once she learns the truth about me, we may never have another.

She runs her hands up my T-shirt and warms herself over my skin. I pull her in tight, and she jumps up on my waist, wrapping her legs around me as if I were a life raft—her lips never leaving mine. We indulge in the pull and push of ecstasy like I have never experienced before—the hard-on blooming in my jeans can attest to that. A series of soft groans emit from her and it takes everything in me not to ride my hands up her shirt—not to take her greedily in the back of my truck, if she wanted me to, and something tells me she more than wants to.

Baya reaches down and plays with the button on my jeans, and I catch her hand in flight.

"No," I whisper, dotting her lips with a kiss.

"Yes," she pants trailing her molten hot lips to my ear then pausing.

"No way," I insist, soft as a whisper.

She gives a little sigh over my lips and it makes me dizzy. "You're off the hook for now, but I want this." She pulls her finger up my belly in a solid line, and I take a breath and seal it in my lungs.

"You hardly know me." A dull laugh brews in my chest as I spin her gently with my hands tucked beneath her knees.

"Hardly know you?" She averts her eyes and I'd do just about anything to please her any way she likes but I know the damage I'm capable of. "*Right*—you have one-night stands all the time. And, I know exactly how many." She taps my chest, resisting the urge to laugh. "Your wall whispered all of your secrets to me this morning while you were in the shower." Baya tries to hide a smile, and I nibble on her lower lip before pulling away.

"I'm not having a one-night stand with you, Baya." True as God. If I had Baya one night would never be enough. "We're just kissing buddies nothing more."

There. Somehow I managed to set a boundary—not that my dick agrees.

"Buddies, huh?" She reaches down and strokes my hard-on over my jeans, and I lurch into her. I've never felt so damn turned on, so ready to come with such little effort. "Your pants feel awful friendly."

"They're not, and neither am I," I tease as a light rain starts to fall.

"Let's get back to the kissing." She pulls her lips across my cheek down to my mouth. "We can figure the rest out later."

Baya lands her candy sweet mouth over mine, and everything in me feels as if it's floating on air. It's as if Baya's kisses were the exact elixir I've been waiting for all these years, a salve in the form of another sweet girl reminiscent of the one I lost.

I've hung out in the dark for so long, I've forgotten what it really feels like to live, to soar with the promise of something wonderful on the horizon.

Baya just might be the light at the end of this long, hellish tunnel. But does she really have the power to pull me from the wreckage? I doubt it. I'm too far gone, too much of a fucking mess to ever hope to recover.

The rain starts in, heavy and hard, matching the rhythm of my heart over hers.

I hope to God, Baya is the cure to this disease I've been wasting away from because it feels like I'm about to die, or at least it did just before I met her.

Her tongue knifes over mine in strokes of lust-driven madness, and I'm right there with her. Not another person on the planet exists right now, not Cole, not a thousand faceless girls from Whitney Briggs—and not the one I left behind in the past.

Right now, it's just Baya and me, drowning in a sea of kisses that taste and feel like the sweetest release. They feel like hope. And, for the first time in a good long while, I have it.

I push Baya up against the truck, and we indulge in the hot of one another's mouths until the sun illuminates a new day with its feather soft beams.

Baya Brighton is in my life, and, now, nothing will ever be the same.

3

Eyes Wide Open

Baya

On Wednesday, after U.S. History and just before American Lit, Laney snags me off the lawn, and we head over to Hallowed Grounds for a cup of something hot to warm our frozen bones. It's hardly the end of September, and already the air is crystalizing into an arctic chill. The leaves have yellowed, and it's a startling effect against the backdrop of the pale blue granite of the mountains, the supple verdant pines.

"So dish," Laney says as we wait for our coffee. Her milky blue eyes are a stark contrast to her long, dark hair, her pale as paper skin. She's pretty in a haunting way.

I fill her in on where I've been spending my nights.

"So, basically, staying with those two is like minoring in Sexology." I twist a lock of hair around my finger while picturing a very naked, very sweaty Bryson panting over me. "Did I just make up a new major?"

"Sexology, huh? I bet you'd like to minor in Bryson Edwards." She purrs into the idea. "I'm sort of majoring in vibrators at the moment. Did I just say that out loud? God

I hate my ex." She shakes the thought away. "Anyway, I'd help you out, but I've got two roommates too many at the moment. So"—she leans in and bites down over her Russian red lips—"on a scale of one to bed, how interested are you in Bryson?"

"Well—he took me to the Sky Lab last weekend." I artfully evade the question with a fact. "That place was all stainless steel and glass. I was completely dizzy by the end of the night." I leave out the fact it was Bryson's kisses, the physical act of him twirling me while his tongue probed the landscape of my mouth that actually caused my head to spin.

"And?" Her pale eyes peer under her bangs, and she looks serious as shit while awaiting an answer.

"*And,* I assure you, no vibrators were harmed during the course of our evening." The only thing vibrating against me was Bryson, and God knows he sent my insides quivering right down to my penis pocket—not that I've ever put anything in it that even remotely resembled a penis. "Maybe we shared a kiss." The sweet memory of that hot exchange wafts through my mind, and my girl parts spasm just thinking about his hands roaming over me. I loved the way his embrace was gentle at times—hard and forceful at others. Who needs the battery response squad when you've got Bryson and his biceps to keep your vagina entertained? Not that he entertained the lower half, but still. Swear to God, if he were here my panties might spontaneously combust. Just thinking about him has me sitting in a puddle. "Okay, it may have been one, *long,* smoking hot kiss."

"He *kissed* you?" She gives an open mouthed moan as if it were the sweetest thing. And it is because, for one, he doesn't require double A batteries.

Once our lattes are ready, we head over to the pot-bellied stove, glowing with a crackling fire. The scent of fresh cut wood bites through the air, penetrating the thick scent of coffee, and the combination makes me heady.

A girl with long auburn hair waves a hand, and Laney speeds us in her direction.

"Baya, this is Roxy." She nods over at the gorgeous Goth-like girl. "She hates people. Roxy—Baya." Laney pulls out a seat, and we join her at the tiny table. Roxy has long, dark hair, more of a chestnut color with magenta highlights, and her eyes illuminate her face a lemony hazel. She's beyond gorgeous, and a part of me wonders if she's a tally mark on Bryson's wall. And for that speculative reason alone, I secretly dislike her. A lot.

"I don't hate people." Her lips curl at the thought. "I hate people with penises."

"Nice." I muse. And I sort of like her better after that misanthropic comment. It takes the edge off any jealous feelings I was ready and willing to nurture.

"Roxy is the resident baker at Whitney Briggs." Laney holds a hand out to her as if making a formal introduction. "She specializes in all things delicious, including penis cupcakes so I suggest you buddy up. This girl has the potential to keep us in cake pops for life."

Roxy wags a finger. "I prefer the term balls on a stick. The blue ones are my favorite." She cuts a hard look at the poor boys sitting across from us.

Okay, I like her a whole lot, now that I know she's more into skewering Bryson's assets than licking them. I give her a wide brimming smile.

Laney peers over the mound of books on the table. "You have anything tall, dark, and chocolate lurking on your plate?"

"Not today." Roxy clears the area to make room for our drinks. "Besides, I have a feeling any baking I do will be few and far between this year. They remodeled the commons area over the summer and took the kitchen out in favor of a pool table. Now I'll have to beg the caf to let me use the facility."

"Sounds like it's back to the Easy Bake for you." Laney gives a brief frown.

"So, what's new?" Roxy takes a sip of her coffee and nods into Laney.

"The drama department is putting on Les Mis, and I'm thinking about auditioning for the part of Fantine."

"*Oh!*" Roxy's face puckers dramatically. "Death and dying in the land of the miserable. Can we get free tickets?"

"Don't you always?"

"That sounds like fun," I say. Laney is so gorgeous it's hard to believe she wouldn't get the part. I glance back at the redhead across from me as if Roxy were coming into focus. She looks more than a little familiar. "Hey, I think you're in my building—Prescott Hall?" I tilt into her. "You're the one with a poster of a cat that tells me to F off on the way to my room." Or at least it did while I was still residing at the palace of perversion, but I leave that part out.

"Correction, old room." Laney pulls her chin back. "She's shacking up with *Bryson Edwards*."

Roxy looks impressed as hell as if I've pulled off the roommate coup of the century. "Does his harem know about this?"

"Technically, I'm crashing with my brother Cole." I glance to Laney. "And, to be honest, I don't really care what Bryson's harem might think." True story. "Bryson and I are just buddies. And I'm quoting."

"*Ooh!*" Laney perks to life at my battle cry. "Sounds like we went from a hot kiss to cold shoulder in a single bound." Her dark brows swoop in like bats in flight. "You know he's a notorious playboy, right? I wouldn't bother pining for him. A leopard like Bryson can't change his spots for anyone."

"Can't or won't?" I'm not sure which is worse.

"Both." Laney nods as if she knows him well enough to attest to his stance on commitment.

"That's too bad." I twirl the warm cup in my hand. "I mean, that kiss we shared was amazing." It was like one long strung out orgasm that's left my entire body throbbing for the past few days.

"Kiss as in *singular*?" Laney looks suspicious. "I've seen that boy in action. I don't think that's possible."

ADDISON MOORE

"Oh, it is," I'm quick to assure her of Bryson's tongue twisting superpowers. "After the bar closed, we indulged in one, long, never-ending kiss that greeted the sun when it finally showed up. We sat right there in that parking lot for hours. It was magic."

"Oh, hon"—Laney grimaces into the thought—"there's a lot of false magic in the parking lot of a bar at three in the morning." She says it with a heavy heart as if she knew firsthand. "He was probably feeling you out to see if he was about to get lucky."

"And I would have happily let him." I take a careful sip of my coffee as an image of me sitting naked on the hood of his truck blips through my mind. The list of things we could have done in that parking lot is endless. "But, the truth is, that kiss was sort of hard won. I practically had to beg. I guess he's just not that into me."

Laney and Roxy exchange looks before breaking out in a laugh.

"Have you *seen* yourself?" Laney's eyes expand like silver dollars. "You're a freaking brunette version of Barbie. Half the girls in Prescott Hall breathed a sigh of relief last weekend because they can finally bring their boyfriends around again."

"Yeah, right." I glance at the ceiling. "Half the girls at Prescott couldn't pick me out of a line up."

"Laney's right." Roxy leans in. "I'd question if Bryson's dick were in working order if he wasn't into you. Besides, I've seen the skanks he's bedded, and trust me it's not an impressive list. You're like the Holy Grail

82

compared to the slut spectacular he's been starring in for years. Of course, he'd want you."

"I'd like to think so, but a part a me just doesn't believe it's true."

A blonde in skin-tight jeans and tall furry boots saunters in. She's got on a giant fuzzy hat that looks as if she shoved a rabbit's ass over her head and a tiny silk scarf sits neat around her neck like a choker. I recognize her from our bizarre early morning encounter the other day—Bryson's latest not-so-greatest bed buddy, Jules.

"Speaking of skanks he's bedded," I whisper as she speeds on over.

"*Saya?*" Her dark eyes round out as she narrows in on me. Her sickly sweet perfume clots up the air, dowsing all the oxygen out of the room.

"Baya," I correct.

"I don't really care what your name is." Her jaw clenches, and her entire head shakes like she's eighty. "You missed the first day of rush and made me look like an a-s-s. Do you want in at Alpha Chi or not?"

"*Y-e-s.*" The thought of witnessing the parade of tramps walk in and out of my brother's bedroom all semester makes my stomach turn. Not to mention the vocal effects that have seeped into my nightmares. The *oohs*, the *ahhs*, the *right there, faster, please* and *thank you*, and my all-time favorite *fuck me like a roadside bitch*. And don't even get me started on the screams and giggles, the moans and groans. I've dreamed of dying barn animals for three nights in a row. Thank God Bryson's penis has voluntarily issued a cease and desist order to females everywhere while I'm squatting on their couch, or I'd literally go insane.

Jules sharpens her chocolate chip eyes at me. "The next meeting is Saturday night at nine. Don't *even* think of missing it. Alpha Chi needs you, and an Alpha never lets her sisters down." She turns on her fuzzy heels and makes a beeline out the door.

"Alpha Chi *needs* you, *Saya,*" Laney mocks. "For the record, Jules Flannery is a j-o-k-e. I may have to disown you if you cross over to the dark side."

"Bryson didn't seem to think she was a j-o-k-e when she tumbled out of his b-e-d." I chew on the inside of my cheek as an image of the two of them mattress dancing clouds my mind. "Anyway, she had it backward, *I* need *them.* My roommate at Prescott is having marathon sex with real live human vibrators, and I can't get any work done with all that grunting—her hairy ass suitors *waving* at me while she bounces on their laps. We're talking serious trampoline action—emphasis on the tramp."

Laney and Roxy laugh until tears roll down their cheeks. It's nice to know they're easily entertained.

"I would have paid to see your face!" Roxy mimics the douchebag waving.

"Believe me, it's not worth the price of admission," I lament. "Besides, she's been nothing but inconsiderate— even *he* took a little time out of the thigh thumping to acknowledge my presence. She hasn't bothered to say good morning *once*—well, at least not with her lips. I've sort of made friends with the Pointer Sisters—Thing One and Thing Two. They're more than friendly with me."

Roxy lights up the place with a high-pitched cackle.

Laney leans in with an incredulous look on her face. "You *named* them?"

"I had to. It was getting lonely, and it was like they're always trying to get my attention. They're like two bloated puppies, happy to see me."

Laney joins Roxy in the laugh fest once again, and any moment now I expect a puddle of urine to form around them.

I guess I could see why they find my relationship with another girl's boobs slightly amusing, only I don't feel like doubling over and slapping the table silly at the moment. The only thing I feel like slapping silly is Jeanie.

"*Baya*." Laney dabs the tears from her eyes with her pinkies. "I can see why you've lost your mind and think Alpha Chi is some kind of Godsend, but it's like six blocks from *Bryson*. If you want to land Edwards, you need to keep in close proximity to him and his penis. I think you should thank the Pointer Sisters for putting you in a prime position."

"I totally agree." Roxy shakes her head emphatically. "I mean, think of the possibilities involved when taking up the same living space. Have you had an 'accidental' run-in after a shower?"

"No." Although the thought of a dripping wet Bryson makes my mouth water. I can see his rippling chest with water beading over it, slowly running tracks to the defined

V just above his forbidden forest of pleasure while he precariously holds his towel just before it drops to his feet.

I catch a breath.

Laney shakes her head. "Any late night chats by the fire?"

"They don't have a fireplace," I'm quick to point out. "Besides he'll get sick of me if I stay there forever. It'll take away the air of mystery we've got going." I reflect on this for a moment. "A little too much mystery if you ask me. Personally I'd like to see his Hardy boys solve a few mysteries with my Nancy Drew."

"Very funny but you're getting bogged down with details." Laney snips. "I think the problem here is he sees you as his best friend's little sister. You need to cure him of that and fast."

"Little sister syndrome." Roxy nods into this as if it were a real disorder. "You'd better step up your game. That's a hard one to break."

"Step up my game," I repeat.

"Less clothes, more talking," Laney says it stern, like an order. "Sexy talking."

"It's called *flirting*." Roxy over enunciates as if I were from another planet and right about now it feels like it. The planet Pluto to be exact which, ironically, the solar system relegated to little sister status not too long ago. I can see myself now on the lunar-like landscape sitting in a pile of rainbow-colored vibrators. God knows there aren't enough batteries in the universe to quench this ache Bryson has set off deep inside me.

"Flirting." I let out a sigh. Truthfully I hadn't really done any of that, not sure I know how. Suddenly a book boyfriend doesn't sound like such a bad idea.

"If he doesn't know you're interested, he might think it's a red light." Laney holds a finger in the air. "I bet Cole threatened to twist his balls off if he even *looked* in your direction."

"Cole did mention something to him when I first arrived—but Bryson *kissed* me. So that sort of debunks that ball-twisting theory." Then again, Bryson did refer to us as "kissing buddies" which sounds like a significant downgrade from "fuck buddies," both of which somehow leave a platonic aftertaste in my mouth.

Laney straightens in her seat. Her face bleaches out.

"*What*?" Both Roxy and I sing it out like a chorus.

"Has he mentioned anything about his past?" She presses her lips tight as if sealing up the damning evidence.

"*No*," I say it so fast it sounds like a chirp. "Why? Should he?"

Laney cuts a look to Roxy. "Only when he's ready." She cinches her backpack over her shoulder and picks up her coffee. "I'd better run. I'm going to be late for Sociology."

I clamp onto her wrist before she can make another move. "What happened in his past that was so terrible?" All sorts of wild scenarios fly through my brain—weapons of mass destruction, a secret divorce, whips and chains...Although that last one I sort of approve of.

"I've known Bryson since we were kids." Laney shakes her head. "There are some things he's just not ready to talk about." She bites down on her lip, and a bloom of grief takes over her features. "Look, go easy on him. When he's ready, *if* he's ready, I'm sure he'll tell you everything." She frees her wrist from my grip. "And, if he does—that means you're pretty special. I haven't heard him talk about the past...well, ever." She takes a step. "Just flirt with him. Most guys just want to have fun, and he'd be insane if he didn't want to have fun with you."

She takes off just as a flicker of lightning ignites outside the window.

"Storm's coming." Roxy takes a deep breath. "Look, don't worry too much about his past. Whatever it is, it's history. You can be his future, Baya. Just let him know you're interested." She picks up her coffee and gives a quick wave before taking off.

I could be Bryson's future. I like the sound of that.

Baya and Bryson. It has a nice ring to it.

I hope he thinks so, too.

❧

By the time I finish up with my classes and head to the apartment, both Cole and Bryson are watching TV, and, unfortunately, each of them has a skanky plus one on the couch with them. Just craptastic.

I give a little wave as I stand awkwardly in the doorway, suddenly feeling like a fifth wheel. Literally.

Cole is stretched out on one couch with a buxom blonde draped over him like a blanket. Bryson and a dark-haired girl that I swear is in my music appreciation class take up the other, although they're sitting less than an arm's length apart. She's pretty in a tragically obvious way—tanned, toned, paper white teeth that go off and on like flashlights as she laughs at the television.

"Want to watch a movie?" Cole nods over to me.

"What movie?" I feign interest as I make my way across the room.

"*Aliens and Indians.* It's a classic, right up there with *Gone with the Wind.*" He casually taps his gal pal over the bottom with a nice crisp slap as if to annunciate his point.

"Nice," I whisper.

Cole has always had an odd fascination with aliens, so I don't see why his cinematic comparison surprises me. He used to be all about the X-Files, but now it's all about the *Sex*-Files. "Sure. I'll change real quick and be right back." I take a moment to scrutinize the fashion sense, or rather nonsense, on display by team estrogen.

Interesting. Both skanks are dressed to impress with nary the storm front in mind. It's obvious those boob-hugging tank tops, the skintight minis, are meant to foster hard-ons more than they are to keep anyone toasty as the weather takes a turn for the nasty. The only thing about to get nasty around here is them. I glance over at the girl glued to Bryson's side with her heavily-lined eyes and eyebrows that look as if they were penciled in by a clown at the fair. Two can play at that game.

I head into the bathroom and dump my makeup bag on the counter until it turns into a pile of MAC vomit, producing enough calk and color to transform me into a guaranteed runner up at Miss Transvestite U.S.A.

A pair of false eyelashes I bought last year at Halloween, mock me. They have a thread of tinsel in them, but it's so damn dark in the living room, I doubt anyone will notice. I pluck them out of their casing and spend a small eternity adhering them to my lids. Hmm... I look...interesting—um...*defined*. Oh, hell, I look downright scary. I take off my Whitney Briggs sweatshirt and dig into my duffle bag until I produce a skimpy lace tank and my barely-there jean shorts I accidentally on purpose swiped from Jeanie-with-the-wienie-obsession. It's not like I really meant to steal them. If I didn't fear a gangbang was imminent, I wouldn't have left in such a damn hurry. Anyway these Daisy Dukes are sort of my good luck charm because I happened to be wearing them last Friday night when Bryson and I engaged in a Guinness worthy lip-lock.

I trade my sensible nude colored bra for my shiny black push up that makes my boobs feel as if they're standing on the edge of a very tall building while my nipples peer over the ledge with that one-eyed look of terror. I throw on the lace top and saunter out of the bathroom while the girls bounce in rhythm. I bet they're offended that I haven't bothered to name them like I did Jeanie's. Desperate One and Desperate Two sounds about right but, sadly, doesn't have a fun ring to it.

I reenter the living room only to find that the bimbo next to Bryson has made herself comfortable with her legs draped over his lap while she greedily lays her head on a throw pillow. I so would have let him have the pillow. She lifts her leg and her foot starts to wander up his chest, climbing further north until she's casually relaxed her thigh over his shoulder—sort of giving him a perverse hug with her knee.

"Take a seat." Cole motions me to the floor in front of the television as if I were a three-year-old, but I turn down his offer and strategically land myself on the lounger across from Bryson.

"You can't see anything from there." Cole frowns over at me as if he's genuinely concerned about my movie experience. Little does he know I'm facing in the right direction to satisfy my viewing pleasure.

"I can see just fine." I glance at the T.V. Actually, he's right. I can't see shit. But what I *can* see is the brunette bimbo giving Bryson a massage with her freshly manicured toes. *Eww*. Her left leg has meandered as well, and her knee has precariously placed itself over the zipper of his jeans. She's flexible, I'll give her that. Her legs are wide open, her skirt is hiked up rather ingloriously around her hips, and, from this vantage point, it looks as if her pink G-string is flossing her in all the wrong places. My gaze floats up his chest, to his blessed by God face, and oh—he's staring right at me. His cheek cinches up one side, and he raises a finger as if he's waving, so I give a little wave back and feel silly in the process.

Crap.

I sink in my seat and revert my attention to the movie just as an alien unhinges its jaw and swallows an unsuspecting Indian chief whole.

My face burns with heat. I wish an alien would swoop down and swallow *me* whole.

Shit. Bryson *saw* me. Even worse he saw me checking out his gal pal's love canal, and now he probably thinks I'm playing for the other team. Stupid Cole for even implying it a few weeks back—and even more stupid me for substantiating his theory by engaging in a crotch watch.

Cole leans up on his elbows and peers over.

"What the hell's that thing hanging off your face?" He leans in further to inspect me. "Dude, you got a bug on your eye?"

I glare at him for a moment. Note to self, embarrass the living shit out of Cole Brighton, soon and often.

"It's nothing." I sink further into my seat and glance over at the exit as if I were planning an Alcatraz worthy escape.

The blonde draped over my brother looks into me with a blank face. "Who is she?" Her hair lies over his forehead, and it looks as if Cole is wearing a bad Halloween wig.

"That's my little sis." There's a sense of pride in his voice when he says it—the kind you reserve for the family pet.

"*Aww!*" The blonde sits up and coos into me as if I had morphed into an infant. "And those fake eyelashes are *so* cute!" She brings her hand to her chest as if I've touched her on an emotional level. "So, like, what grade are you in?"

Grade? "I'm a freshman," I'm quick to apprise her of my quasi-adult standing.

"Really?" She gawks at me as if it were impossible. "I would have thought you were a lot younger. I have a sister in junior high, and you sort of remind me of her."

Just crap.

The brunette molesting Bryson with her kneecap leans forward. "You have some lipstick right here." She points just under her nose. "I wasn't going to say anything, but it's not like you're trying to impress anyone." She strums her fingers across his chest like an afterthought. "You know, if you ever want tips on how to do your makeup, I could totally teach you. I have about nine tutorials up on YouTube right now. You should check them out." She looks over at Bryson. "I love playing with makeup. Plus it helps with my modeling."

Great. I've just been reduced to a seventh grader, and *she's* a model. I sink in my seat until my bottom actually slips off the edge and watch the remainder of Aliens and Indians until my ass goes numb.

After the movie, Cole sends the blonde packing to his bedroom with a firm squeeze to her behind, and she giggles her way down the hall. I'm sure she's amped up just thinking of all the loving, touching, squeezing about to take place.

Bryson and the super model hit the fridge, probably to load up on carbs they'll soon burn up in his bedroom, and I'm left in the living room all by my clown-faced lonesome. Suddenly going back to Prescott Hall and watching Jeanie engage in a series of naked calisthenics doesn't sound like such a bad idea. In fact, I'd rather subject my brain to her sexual performance piece than watch Bryson score a homerun with a runway model.

Cole barrels toward me with his dimples depressed in a frown.

"What's going on?" There's a tenderness in his voice that I hadn't heard since I've touched down in North Carolina. It's the phone-call version of my brother. The one I'm far more used to, even though he was nothing but a lie.

"Nothing's going on." I cross my arms over my chest in an effort to hide my cleavage. It's like I've got my boobs set at the right trajectory to launch to the moon, and he's the last person I'd want to witness the intergalactic event.

"Get some clothes on, would you? I get it. You want to get comfortable before bed. But I don't want anyone seeing you like this. You're practically naked." He glances over his shoulder at Bryson and his pop tart of the night. "There's a pervert on the loose, and I don't want him to get the wrong message." He pulls me into a long, strong hug.

"Yeah, well"—I shoot a look to Bryson who currently has his back to me—"the pervert has a hot date. I seriously doubt he notices I'm even in the building."

"Good. Let's keep it that way." He tousles my hair and gives a wry smile. "Night kiddo."

"Goodnight." I watch as Cole struts into the hall with his bad boy swagger.

Bryson and his gal pal stride toward the exit. "Goodnight!" She waves over at me. "Get in touch with me if you ever want to learn to do your makeup. You should never just slop it on like that."

What's this? The star of Bryson's bedroom rodeo is calling it a night? She whisks her makeup loving, catwalk strutting self right out the door, and Bryson seals it in what I'd like to think is a good riddance kind of way. Doubtful.

"She left in a hurry." I head over to the fridge and pluck out a water bottle. "Big shoot in the morning?" I don't know why I went there. It's probably true.

"Maybe." He gives a sideways grin and joins me at the breakfast counter. "But I wouldn't really know. I told her I was tired." His silver eyes ride up and down my features, and I can feel his gaze as it travels over every inch, heavy and wanting. "What's with the—?" He motion in a circle around his face.

"Oh..." I bite down hard on my bottom lip to keep from spontaneously bursting into tears. Here I was a trying to seduce him, and I've only made myself look ridiculous.

"You look pretty." He pushes his shoulder into mine playfully. "And, for the record, you don't need it. You're a natural beauty."

My body bisects with heat. One day I'm going to spontaneously combust, and it'll all be Bryson Edwards' fault.

"Thank you." I lean in a little in the event his investigative efforts decide to drift south, but they don't. It's becoming clear as the fake eyelash that just floated down from my face that Bryson thinks of me as nothing more than Cole's kid sister. "So, tell me something about you. I mean, I showed you the girls the second I got on campus, surely that must entitle me to some rudimentary information other than your first and last name." Crap. A sinking feeling settles in my chest. I totally forgot he's harboring some deep dark secret from yesteryear.

"I like to cook."

"Really?" My insides loosen as I relax into him.

"No." The smile drops from his face as he shakes his head. "But I do like to eat— ice cream tops the list."

"You like ice cream?" For some reason this dairy connection we're experiencing makes my thighs tingle.

"Am I from the plant earth? Damn straight I like ice cream." That hotter-than-hell smile appears and disappears.

He rounds out the counter and pulls a carton from the freezer.

96

"Vanilla okay?" His cheek slides up one side. "I'm boring that way."

"Vanilla's perfect. And you strike me as a lot of things, but boring isn't one of them."

A part of me wants to bring up that kiss we shared— see if he wants another, but the aftertaste of desperation is already rising to the back of my throat like bile. Bryson kisses a lot of girls. I guess I was just one of them.

Bryson locks his eyes over mine as the grin slides down his face. He's bearing into me, speaking in some code I can't quite decipher. A static charge ignites the air between us as a smile tugs on his lips. His lids dip, and he's bedroom eyeing me for a moment before taking a breath and snapping back to reality.

He quickly busies himself with the task of scooping us each a bowl of ice cream then lures me to the sofa.

"So"—I slide in next to him with my legs crossed beneath me—"what do you do for fun outside of the bars? From what I hear there's a party on Greek row every night and twice on Sunday."

He shakes his head. "Nope, again, I'm pretty boring. Once in a while I'll tag along with your brother, but outside of work, there's not much to me. I try to head home, once or twice a month. I like hanging out with my mom and sister."

I melt a little on the inside. And here I thought he was this insatiable sex god. Well, he was until last weekend, but just the thought of him wanting to hang out with his family makes me want him twice as bad. I imagine his strong hot hands pouring over my body like oil. His heated kisses peppering my neck, behind my ear until he finally finds my lips, and I sigh with approval.

He gives a little smile, and my sweet spot clenches as if waving him in.

"That's really nice." I wish Bryson were some big bully who gave new meaning to fornicating frat boys everywhere, but, he's not, he's a downright nice guy who just so happens to keep a careful accounting of the girls he has his way with.

"You should meet my sister." He tweaks my knee, and a fire rips up my leg, right to that secret place where no man has yet to venture, and my vagina drops to its knees, pleading for me to do something to usher this boy inside. "She's awesome," he continues. "And I know for a fact she'd love you."

"Really?" If I didn't know better I'd say it was a date—the meet the family rendition reserved for girlfriends the world over. "I would love to." Me and my vagina, "Can't wait." His sister would love me? Sure wish her brother would. Maybe that's what I want deep down inside, for Bryson Edwards to fall madly in love with me. My entire body tingles as if nodding in agreement.

My cheeks fill with heat at the idea, and I lower my gaze to the floor. I feel ridiculous just entertaining the idea of Bryson falling for me in that way.

"I'm headed home, weekend after next." He strokes his hand over my thigh in a seemingly innocent pass, but my muscles tremble for him to continue. My nipples perk to attention in the event his fingers dare to venture north. "You want to come with me?"

A breath gets trapped in my throat while my heart tries to evict itself from my chest. He wasn't asking the super model who likes to floss in delicate places to go home with him, or J-u-l-e-s from Alpha Chi Chi—he's asking *me*. But, then again, I shouldn't get my hopes up. He probably wants me to tag along as a play date for his sweet little sis while he and the super model bump and grind all weekend.

"I would love to go." I hear myself say, and it sounds strange, foreign coming from my lips. Am I actually agreeing to go away with Bryson, whose penis has already qualified for the gynecological exploratory finals? Not that I wouldn't mind him exploring my gynecological needs, and God knows I have them.

"Good." He pushes into me, and this time our shoulders stay linked, forming a long line of heat that tunnels right down between my thighs.

He winces. "We might want to hold off on saying anything to Cole." His brows tweak in the direction of my brother's bedroom. "I think he'd rearrange my man parts if he knew."

"I won't say a word," it comes from me slow, seductive. I can't believe I'm going away for an entire weekend with the most gorgeous guy on campus—on the planet, Pluto included. "I kind of like the idea of having a secret from my brother." I bat my lashes into him and note the silver shadow over my left eye. I reach up and pluck it off, and we share a quiet laugh.

We steady our gaze over one another, and the room stills around us. It's as if a fire ignited, rippling its way across all four walls. It's so damn hot that even the tank top and silly micro shorts I'm wearing feel like far too much to have on.

I lean in a little to see if he'll give.

Bryson leans in, matching me inch for inch. His face is stone cold, but I can feel the wanting radiating off his skin like heat off a radiator grill.

"Kiss me," I whisper. My nipples tighten as if balling themselves in two tiny fists as they cheer me on. The word *please* is just about to leap from my lips.

His mouth curves in a devilish grin. Something tells me he loves to see me beg.

A door rattles in the hall, and Bryson leans back, deep into the couch.

Cole's blonde bimbo tiptoes to the bathroom wearing nothing but a tank top that she's holding over her freshly spanked bottom. Swear to God she's sporting a handprint on her left thigh.

No sign of my overprotective big bro. Clearly this was a false alarm. And now I'll never get that kiss.

"Goodnight, Baya." Bryson gives his signature sad smile as he taps the wall on his way to bed.

"Night." I call after him unable to control my elation.

Bryson wants me to spend an entire weekend with him, and my girl parts and me are already counting down the days.

Bryson

Saturday afternoon, on what's panning out to be the final weekend we might see the sun for the next ten months, Holt invites us out on his boat.

"*Hey.*" Cole nods over as I'm busy filling the cooler with water and beer. "Baya thinks she's going." He looks pissed at the thought.

"That's because I invited her." I took her to the Black Bear last night, and she wanted a kiss after closing again, but I kindly shut her down. I made up some crap excuse about having to work on some internship bullshit, and she bought it, mostly. The truth is, I wanted that kiss as bad as she did, if not more. I wanted to dive into her mouth and run my tongue over every inch of her body right there in the back of my truck if she'd let me, but I can't bring myself to do it. I'd take her down in grand style, and I'll never be able to live with myself if I do. It's not fair to Baya, and it's not fair to Steph.

"*Un*invite her." Cole drills into me with those sage green eyes that he hooks the girls with. "I've got Taylor double D Diggs coming, and we both know she's not shy about where she parties."

"Sounds like your blowjob on the sea just got blown out of the water."

"It's a lake, moron."

"You're the moron. I'm not telling her she can't go."

Baya walks into the room with a hot pink bikini on and, holy shit, not one stitch more. Her tits melon out, nice and round, and her legs ride up from her high heels like two creamy stems that keep on going. I've been jacking off in the shower every night this week thanks to the glorious stages of undress she's been teasing me with, but she's just taken my hard-on to a whole new level.

"It's freezing out." Cole snatches the towel from her hand and wraps it around her body like he's concealing criminal evidence. "Throw on some sweats or something. Would you?" He spins her toward the bathroom. "And a scarf and some gloves. You don't want your fingers falling off."

I give a little chuckle. I guess I'd feel the same way with Annie if the roles were reversed. Just the thought of Cole even looking at my sister that way gets my blood pumping. I'm starting to see his point—another good reason for me to stay the hell away from Baya Brighton.

An inferno scorches my insides at the thought.

I'm pretty sure the last thing I'm going to do voluntarily is stay away. The only thing I really want to do is be with her twenty-four seven. My heart aches because I've never felt that strongly about anyone before. And I can't help but wonder if I'm hurting Steph all over again.

The lake is unseasonably warm. Holt has some girl in a G-string already seated on his lap. We exchange brief hellos as I walk down the dock. It's not until I help Baya onto the boat that I notice there are three other girls laying out on the bow. Crap. The boat's not that big. I was sort of hoping Holt and Cole would keep the girls to one a piece so Baya and I could team up by proxy and get a chance to talk.

We settle in and Baya does her best to fit in with the girls, but, for the most part, they seem to be ignoring the fact she's politely peppering the conversation. It's cool. I mean they don't know her. So it'll only make sense when I hang out with her. Cole can't fault me for that.

We finally take off, and Holt settles the boat mid-lake before he starts dispensing beer bottles like they were oxygen tanks that everyone on board needed to survive. Baya passes, and I do, too. Funny how she hates the taste of liquor, and Cole seems to think it's nectar from the gods. Baya and Cole seem to be opposite in just about every single way. It just goes to show how two people could be raised under the same roof and have a totally different outlook on things, sort of like Holt and me. It's strange how Cole has never mentioned his father's accident. It must have been a trauma. Speaking of traumas, Steph has eroded the inside of my brain every single day since that fateful night, and I don't think Holt has thought of her twice since the incident. Holt had a Steph phase once, but you wouldn't know it.

I head out to the bow, and the girls break out in a choir of catcalls. The sticky haze seeps over my skin as I shoot a quiet smile at Baya. She's so beautiful. She makes every other girl on the boat evaporate in the fog around her. My heart thumps as I take her in.

"It's time to get this party started!" Holt's girlfriend for the afternoon turns up the radio full tilt as she and her friends strip down to their bathing suits—fuck—more like birthday suits.

I swallow hard—every single one of them has on a G-string.

Baya shoots me a look, and I hold out my hands a moment, trying to remove myself from the situation. If I knew a mass disrobing was about to take place I would never have come, and, for sure, I wouldn't have brought Baya.

"Nice!" Cole slaps me on the back and pulls Taylor to the side while she eagerly works the button on his jeans.

Holt goes over and sits among the bevy of bronzed wannabe beauties and wraps his arms around two different girls.

Shit. This is turning into the love boat, and I'm betting Baya wishes she could abandon ship. I nod her over, and we sit at the wheel with Baya taking up the captain's seat.

"So it's a pleasure cruise." She gives a sly smile, and I tick to life in my boxers. Baya is the hottest girl on the lake even with her Whitney Briggs sweats, her fresh scrubbed face, her cute as hell ponytail.

Cole lets out a serious groan, and Baya winces as if she were in real pain.

"Honest to God." I hold up a hand. "If I knew, I never would have asked you."

The smile slides off her face. Her eyes elongate in two perfect orbs.

"Please"—she shakes her head—"don't let me stand in your way. Go on, help yourself to the buffet while I steer us into the nearest boulder." She plucks a deck of playing cards off the dash and waves them in front of me. "Never mind. I found something to keep me busy. I'll keep my hands off the wheel I promise." She tries her best to shoo me away. "I'll be fine. You don't need to babysit me." It comes out curt, pissed as hell, as she shuffles the cards with a marked aggression.

"Hey"—I lay my hand over hers—"for the record, I wish it was just me and you on this boat." Right now there is no greater truth. I lean in and whisper just over her ear. "I'm sorry I put you through this."

Her jade eyes settle on mine, and I want to damn both Cole and any memory of the past to hell and kiss her right here.

"Nice try," she whispers, laying out a row of cards in front of her. "I've seen the one in the red bikini blow you kisses *twice*. Now leave." She nods over to the bow. "The last thing I want to do is get in the way of your tally marks."

Baya blinks back tears, and my chest feels like it's about to implode. Shit. In an effort to keep her heart safe, I've started to break it.

"What if I told you I wasn't into tally marks anymore?" I lean in and hold her gaze.

Baya looks down at my lap like she's fearing for the boys, then slowly rides her smoldering eyes toward mine. There's a heat between us like I've never felt with anyone before, not the hundreds of girls that drifted through my bedroom, not with Steph, and I feel guilty as hell for even thinking it.

"No tally marks, huh? Switching to an electronic scoreboard?" Her lips twitch. "I bet there's an app for that."

"Nope." I match her steady gaze and neither of us moves. "I think I'll hold out for something better—someone special."

"Someone special." She swallows hard as her eyes expand at the idea.

I hope Baya knows she's that someone special.

I think that's exactly what I'm about to discover.

We play twenty-one for the next few hours. And I'm slowly starting to realize it's Baya who's quickly becoming the queen of my heart.

4

Into Your Arms

Baya

Alpha Chi is lit up like a haunted house against the backdrop of a veiled starry night. The ground clouds skirt the edges of the gargantuan McMansion, giving it that ethereal feel, and, suddenly, it looks as though I'm stepping into a dream.

"You sure you want to do this?" Laney reapplies her poppy red lipstick, never once taking her eyes off the overgrown estate.

"I'm positive. The sooner I can switch off the I-Wet-Dream-of-Jeanie show, the better. Besides, who wouldn't want to live in a haunted mansion?" I pull her up the steps.

"I still think you're making a really huge mistake. From what you said about this afternoon, you're making some serious strides with your current roommate."

"Yeah, well, like I said, Bryson is a nice guy. He probably just felt bad that I was the only girl on the boat who didn't get the 'wear your thong memo.' Besides, I doubt a card game equals serious strides." He never did mention that kiss—but, then again, neither did I.

Laney pulls me back by the shoulder and twists her crimson lips into me.

"You don't believe that for a minute, and neither do I. Face it, that boy has a hard-on with your name on it. If Bryson Edwards said he wished you were the only two people on that boat, I'm betting he meant it. I don't think he's done a lot of articulating with the girls he's been with. He's more of a get right down to brass mattress tacks kind of guy."

A spiral of heat spears through me at the idea of Bryson wanting me that way. I've yet to see his bedroom, but I totally envision a golden bed with a holy light emanating from above while a choir of angels sing a chorus of hallelujah.

"We'd better make this quick," I whisper as we come upon the giant glass doors. "We've got a shift to pull in less than an hour." Bryson asked if I wanted to work the Black Bear, and of course I said yes.

A crystal chandelier blossoms from the ceiling, and I peer inside before bothering to knock. Dark expansive floors bleed throughout the downstairs, and a navy carpet runs up the steps, held back with long, gilded bars. An entire crowd of girls have amassed in the great room just beyond the entry, and one of them spots us and motions us inside. They're all dressed in black tea length dresses with their hair neatly coifed and... eerily they're all wearing a single strand of pearls. Why do I feel like a sorority version of the clone wars is about to break out?

Laney leans in. "So if we make it, do we have to morph into an Alpha Chi-bot?"

"It's the fashion camaraderie that links them together." It looks more fashion jinx than link, but I keep the commentary to myself.

"I don't know." She shudders in her jean jacket. "Something about the blue oyster cult is really creeping me out."

One of the walking pearls skips over in her heels, creating a grating sound over the floor. "Hi! I'm Lynn. Who's your sponsor?" Her hair is curled under at the ears, and she's in the requisite little black dress with discards from the ocean strung helpless around her neck. Suddenly I'm feeling a wee bit nervous because obviously I didn't get the memo to get my pearls or my perky on—not that I own pearls, and God forbid that I own an ounce of perky.

"She's mine!" Jules rushes over with her blonde mane perfectly twisted in stiff little ringlets.

"Oh my, gosh! You brought a friend!" She spasms over me as if Laney herself were manna from heaven. "Come, come." She pulls us each by the hand and scuttles into the center of the room as if we were exhibit A and B.

"Who is this?" A brassy blonde steps forward, and you can tell by her resting bitch face, that ultra-cruel look in her eyes, that she's the one in charge of this quasi-hostage situation. "And why are they breaking dress code?" She barks at Jules, inspiring her to shrink three inches.

"Relax, Aubree." Laney rolls her eyes. "This is Baya Brighton, and you'd be lucky if she graced your presence."

I'm impressed that Laney knows her, but, then, Laney seems to know everyone and everything about them. Not that she's filling me in on all the dirty little deets.

The queen bee inspects me with a look of slight disgust. Her brassy hair is pulled up high, and she has on enough mascara to give her that spider lash effect. There's a sinister feel to her, so it doesn't surprise me that she's driving this crazy train.

"Did you tell me I'd be *lucky* to have her grace my presence?" Aubree squints into Laney until her eyelashes look as if they want to crawl off her face.

Nobody moves, nobody breathes. Dear God, you would think I slaughtered their mothers the way every girl in the room looks like they want to personally murder me in my sleep.

"Well, Laney and *Baya*"—she growls with a heated disdain—"we have a dress code to abide by. But, since you're obviously clueless, I'll let it slide just this once." She snaps a finger in the air, loud and crisp as if she broke a bone in the process. "All new recruits line up against the back!" Her voice echoes through the room, vibrating the chandelier sconces until they sizzle against the wall. "Welcome to the hall of truth. Here at Alpha Chi we believe that authenticity and integrity are of the upmost value. We never hesitate telling a sister exactly how we feel because the truth is what separates a sister from a friend. For instance"—she glances at the bevy of girls behind her, and the entire lot of them shrink in fear, well, not really but you could see it in their eyes—"when Lynn here got her hair chopped off at a place that specializes in ten dollar hack jobs, I let her know that little follicular fuck-up was going to cost her a place at the next four social events with our matchups at Sigma Theta Tau."

A gasp circles the room while Lynn closes her eyes a moment as if reliving the horror.

"And, when you, Jen"—she flicks a finger at a shorter girl with a mole the size of a dime just under her left eye— "tried to join the a cappella group after I graciously informed you that you sing like shit...." A smile that borders on a snarl graces her face. "Well, why don't *you* tell everyone what happened next?"

"I didn't make it." The girl with the mole gives a hard sniff.

"What's that?" Aubree barks it out like a command.

"I didn't make it! You were right. I sing like a sack of shit on fire, and I defamed the good name of Alpha Chi!" She yelps it out at the crowd as if the reprimand was meant for us all along.

Holy crap. Are these people for real?

"Now"—Aubree gives a soft clap while that stupid wicked smile plays on her lips—"the sisters and I are looking forward to getting to know each of you better. State your name and the reason you'd like for us to consider you as future members of Alpha Chi. Honest answers only." Her eyes reduce to slits, and suddenly I'm fearing for my room at the haunted inn. "I have an exceptional radar for liars." Her thin lips set in a line, and somehow I believe her.

The girls at the far end start in on the fun while Laney leans into me.

"Aubree and I grew up together," she whispers. "She's been hot and bothered over Bryson for as long as I can remember, so I wouldn't mention him—Cole either just to be safe."

I give a barely-there nod. "What do I say?" I zip the words through the side of my lips like a ventriloquist.

"Say that you'd die to live here," she whispers. "That you came to Whitney just for Alpha Chi."

"Excuse me?" The brassy bitch snaps her fingers in our direction. "It looks like someone here likes talking out of turn." Her dark eyes narrow in on us, her jaw roots itself to the ground, incredulous that we even bothered to *breathe* out of turn. I half-expect her to punch us in the throat. "Why don't you two go next since you're so excited, you could hardly keep your pie holes shut. You first." She hardens her gaze at me.

"Baya Brighton, and I would l-o-v-e to become a member of Alpha Chi—" I thought spelling it out would be a cute touch since Jules seems to be addicted to the alphabet. Wait...do I really want to be a member of Alpha Chi and have more of this *f-u-n*?

"Why?" Aubree's eyes expand the size of baseballs. "Spit it out."

Lynn and Jules drape her like bookends, albeit frightened, quaking in their patent stilettos, bookends.

"I would really love to become a member of Alpha Chi..."—now would be a great time to dream up some craptastic answer, but, truthfully, I'm a little short on lies at the moment so I go for the truth—"so I don't have to witness Jeanie Waters fornicating herself into a cardiac episode." Thing One and Thing Two blink through my mind as if they were waving hello.

The room lights up with laughter, and I let out a breath I didn't even know I was holding.

That's a good sign right? Adding levity to the situation and all that good stuff? I can feel a bite of perspiration under my arms because I seriously doubt inciting a laugh riot is a very good fucking sign.

Shit. I can't believe I just said that crap about Jeanie out loud. It was one thing to tell a few people but an entire crowd of questionably stable girls? My mouth has officially morphed into the rumor mill.

"Also"—it's like I'm on autopilot, and my lips won't stop moving—"sharing a bathroom with my brother and his roommate is growing a little old." I manage to leave the parade of sluts out of the equation for now, although Bryson did mention he was handing the keys to the carnal kingdom to my brother.

Aubree narrows her gaze at me. She leans so far in my direction, I'm positive she's about to flop over. Her jaws cut back like razors, her lips are pulled into a thin line of hatred, and I'm pretty sure I've just reduced my stay at this glorified mortuary to zero. Why don't I just tell them I hate tea length dresses and pearls? Or really go out in style and swing a sickle from the second floor balcony while screaming, *die bitches!*

"So let me get this straight?" Aubree takes a few steps toward me, and the room echoes with the click of her heels. "You want to join our sorority because you ran away from your romping roommate? And you don't like the bathroom accommodations at your brother's place?" Her pink glossy mouth contorts in disapproval.

Oh, what the hell. "Yes." I bite down on my lip in an effort to block my vocal cords from spewing any more hardcore truths, but it's no use. "*And*, I happen to hate tea length dresses and pearls." A circle of gasps titter around the room. "This *is* the hall of truth, right?"

She sucks in a breath and darts her finger toward the exit.

ஐ

Laney and I laugh our asses off as we speed over to the Black Bear Saloon.

"You were brilliant." She shakes her head into the dark two-lane highway.

"*So* do you think they'll let us in?" I can't even finish the thought before the two of us hack out another round of good old-fashioned air laughs. Laney swerves momentarily before pulling into the parking lot.

"If they did let us in, I'm pretty sure Alpha Chi would be a lot more fun. Seriously though"—Laney wipes the tears from her eyes with her pinkies—"you'll probably wish you didn't blow rush."

"What are you taking about? That girl had I-specialize-in-breaking-lady-balls written all over her face. There's no way I'll ever regret not scoring a room at the mansion of misery." Well, maybe I'll regret it a little.

"I know, but I was just thinking, you might be right. If things get serious between you and Bry—you know, once you're officially together, you'll want to find someplace else to stay to maintain that air of mystery for a while."

"Officially together," I whisper. Just the thought of being with Bryson sends me soaring. I'd be the envy of every girl at Whitney Briggs. Hell, I'd be the envy of *me*.

Laney and I hop out of the car and head on in. The Black Bear is jammed packed with bodies tonight. Music pulsates through the speakers at lethal decibels, and Holt lifts a drink to us from behind the black granite bar. It's just this side of creepy the way he looks almost exactly like his brother—I guess being fraternal twins will do that. Then I see him—the real deal. Bryson's smile expands as his eyes lock onto mine. His jaw cinches tight. He's got that five o'clock shadow peppering his cut features, and his entire face lights up when he sees me.

"Would you look at that?" Laney muses as she ties on her apron. "He's like a kid on Christmas morning with you around. Looks like someone's about to get l-a-i-d," she sings that last part before disappearing into the crowd.

Right. More like *paid,* as in, by the patrons. At least I can almost guarantee that's going to happen tonight. Not that I would mind getting "laid," but something about the word makes me squirm. I've always envisioned my first time to be in a bubble of perfect love with someone who wanted me as much as I wanted them. And, with Bryson, I feel an emotional push in the opposite direction, I don't know why.

I slip behind the bar and pluck an apron from under the counter.

"Ready for some action?" Bryson curls into me, and, for a moment, I think he's propositioning me.

"Action? I bet half of the girls that come in this place are trying to get lucky with an Edwards brother." I wink as I tie the white frilly apron around my waist.

Holt barks out a laugh, and I startle. I didn't see him swoop on over, really I was referencing one Edwards in particular, that being Bryson.

"Listen, sweetheart"—Holt leans in with that come hither look in his eye—"if you can't find an Edwards brother to pleasure you tonight, track me down at about three in the morning." He socks Bryson in the arm before heading to the other end of the bar.

"That wasn't awkward," I say, mostly to myself.

"If you're in the market for an Edwards brother, I can tell you Holt's the wrong one—unless, of course, you're also in the market for a medication-resilient STD. Then you're free to venture."

"Oh? Does his scoreboard put yours to shame?"

His lids hood over. "The only thing I've scored lately is a clean bill of health per my last physical." A slight dimple goes off on his left cheek. His face looks tan from the boat ride this afternoon, and his stubble has taken over, giving him that hot, scruffy look I'm a sucker for. He leans onto the bar and gazes at me as if he's flirting.

"So"— I swallow hard, never taking my eyes off his— "which Edwards brother is the right one?"

The music cuts out, and a sharp bite of feedback takes over the speakers, inspiring ten different people in the vicinity to cover their ears. A slow song starts in and resettles the mood in the room.

Bryson pinches his lips together, taking me in as if I was dessert, but he doesn't answer the question. Instead, he tilts his head and stares into me dreamily, at least that's the story I'm buying.

"You want to dance?" He nods over to a small clearing between the tables.

"I've never seen anyone dance here before." Heat rises to my cheeks, and I take a breath at the prospect of holding his perfect body to mine.

"I think maybe it's time people start." Bryson clasps onto my fingers and gently threads us through the crowd until we're centered in the tiny clearing. He pulls me in and wraps his arms around my waist, warming me from head to toe with an instant inferno. His knees press against my inner thighs, he intertwines our fingers, and another wave of heat sears through me. Bryson never takes his eyes off mine while his pelvis pushes into me as if giving me the carnal green light.

My throat goes dry. My heart thumps in my ears so loud I swear he can hear it.

I glance up at him starry eyed. Bryson Edwards is the sex god of Whitney Briggs, and he's dancing with me. In. Public.

A group of girls turn their heads in our direction just as a few other couples meander over and dance alongside us.

"Looks like your evil plan worked." I bite down over my lower lip to keep from spewing out any additional suggestions that might work, such as reenacting our moves in a horizontal position sans clothing. God knows that the nightmare at Alpha Chi has unleashed word vomit central in my brain.

"I figured if you're in the market for an Edwards brother, I might as well put my best foot forward— literally." He gives a lopsided grin, and my stomach pinches.

"Yeah, well, you're a pretty good kisser so I'd be a fool not to choose you." What am I saying? *Choose* you? I'm the desperate one, not the other way around. Besides, it was just one kiss—one long, fantastic, mind-blowing lip exchange that will play out in my fantasies until I'm dust and bones, but, nevertheless, he relegated me and my pucker to the buddy rack before the night was through, so there's that. I've practically made a pass at him on three other occasions but he's declined every offer since that magical night. I guess Laney was right, parking lot magic isn't a real thing after all.

"You want to blow this place and go have a good time?" His eyes hood over again, and a surge of adrenaline pulsates in that sweet spot between my legs.

Oh God. What the hell is *good time* code for? Am I really going to sleep with Bryson and become some nameless tally mark on his wall?

A tiny voice that creeps from somewhere deep in my vagina screams a loud, demanding, *hell yes*.

"Sure," I hear myself say. "I'm ready to have all the fun you're willing to give me." *Give me?* I glance down at his chest briefly. Who the hell has taken over my mouth? This is exactly what I swore I would never do, meaningless sex with cute frat boys. Even if he's not a frat boy, the premise is still the same. I want it to mean something. I want Bryson to care about me, to want *me* in more than just a sexual sense—well, ideally anyway. Maybe he feels like the only way to get me off his back is to pin me down with his boy toy and get it over with? And, sadly, he's probably right.

Laney gives a thumbs-up from over his shoulder, and I try not to break out in a goofy grin.

Bryson swivels his hands up over my back, and my insides give a mean quiver. He leans in with his cheek an inch away from mine, and I can feel the heat emanating off his skin in waves. The song wraps up, and he leads me by the hand to the exit, giving Holt a quick wave on our way out the door.

The crisp night air enlivens my senses, and then it hits me—I'm off to who knows where on a Saturday night with Bryson Edwards. And if that doesn't qualify as a date then I don't know what does.

"So where to?" I jump a little at the thought of going anywhere with the god of good times at my side.

"How about we start with dinner?"

⧽⧽⧼⧼

Bryson and I hit a Chinese restaurant down the street, and I tell him all about my misadventure at Alpha Chi over dinner and the fact I still sort of wish I could get in. I leave out the "air of mystery" portion of my argument. But now that we're ditching work for a little alone time, I'm seriously reconsidering that whole air of mystery thing.

His chest thumps with a silent laugh. "You're a non-conformist. I like that. Most girls would have lied, and you told the truth. That's what I like about you—you're so innocent, it's cute."

A slight rail of alarm spirals through me.

"I'm not that innocent." My entire face darkens to the shade of the maroon tablecloth, giving away the fact I totally am. I'm not sure I like the idea of being "cute" either.

"Hey"—he leans over the table and clasps my hand—"there's nothing wrong with being innocent. I swear, I didn't mean it like an insult."

My eyes grow heavy, and I inspect every item on the table because I can't bring myself to look up at him.

"Yeah, well"—my fingers loosen from his grasp—"I guess I'm ready and willing to find someone to defile me." Not really. This all feels so achingly desperate that a part of me wants to run all the back to Prescott Hall and ask one of Jeanie's many bare ass suitors to have their way with me just to take the edge off.

Bryson pulls his sad, pale eyes over me. "Trust me, the last thing you want is for someone to defile you." His glassy eyes roll over mine. He looks serious as death. "Promise me you'll hold out for something better."

Hold out? Sounds like tonight isn't ending with a private wrestling match like I hoped it would.

"What could be better?" I hold my breath a moment as he considers this. Earlier, on the boat, he said he was hanging up the scoreboard, looking for something better. I was sort of hoping that could be me.

Bryson licks his lips. His eyes widen for a moment as if he were about to say something then aborts the effort.

He clears his throat. "I think you should fall in love, Baya." His gaze dips to the table then rides back up over my features. "I think you should fall so head over heels you don't know what's up and what's down anymore. You deserve to be worshiped and cared for. The last person on the planet who deserves you is some kid trolling for a quick hookup. Trust me, you're the most beautiful girl I have ever laid eyes on. You could have your pick of the litter." He bears into me a moment with his steely gaze. "Any guy would be crazy not to want you."

Any guy.... And suddenly it's becoming clear that dinner is just dinner.

A moment thumps by with our eyes never losing their stranglehold on one another. The waiter brings the check and drops a fortune cookie in front of each of us.

"Let's see what the future holds." I give an impish grin as I pop the package open and pull out the cookie. "We're supposed to say 'underneath the sheets' after we read our fortunes, that makes it a lot more fun." And accurate I want to add but don't.

"You first." He rubs his leg against mine, nudging me.

"Okay." I pluck the thin strip of paper out with its tiny red font. "A pleasant surprise is in store for you, *underneath the sheets.*" I hold it up victoriously as a laugh bubbles from my chest. Dear God almighty let this be so. Amen.

"Sounds like a goodtime will be had by all." His brows tweak as he pulls out his fortune. "Conquer your fears or they will conquer you." His expression dims as if that tiny piece of paper had been speaking directly to his heart.

"*Underneath the sheets.*" I give his leg a little kick.

He offers a quiet laugh, but his eyes are still throbbing with grief.

"What has you so afraid, Bryson?" I ask below a whisper. It's becoming painfully obvious that the past is still very much holding him hostage.

His clear eyes dart up to mine. "Maybe it's you."

ଽଓଓଷ

After dinner we hop back in his truck, and Bryson drives us down narrow tree-lined roads as we wind our way up the side of the mountain.

"Witch's Cauldron, okay?" He darts his eyes to me before firming his stare back over the open highway. The fog settles in, and the headlights illuminate the night, blinding and white.

"Sounds great." My heart thumps once unnaturally. That's where we went a few weeks back. It was private and tragically romantic. This time we're short on donuts and coffee, no beautiful sunrise to admire, with only ourselves to keep each other entertained.

Bryson rounds his hand over the steering wheel as we pull in just beneath the pale blue boulders. We get out, and he helps me climb onto the lowest rock that overlooks the hot spring.

"Looks like we're all alone." I scoot into him and take in the night magic that's brewing around us. The pale glow of the moon highlights the water while the pines hover above like guardians that Cole himself sent to protect my virginity. Little does he know Bryson is pretty interested in me keeping it intact for that one special guy as well.

A lone wolf howls from somewhere deep in the forest, and a chill runs up my spine.

"Doesn't sound like we're alone." Bryson gives a dark laugh, low and sexy, but despite my passive reaction I'm scared to freaking death.

Screw it. "God, we're going to get eaten alive." I bounce over and practically land in his lap. "Sorry," I say, sliding off his knee. "I'm not a fan of rabid beasts with sharpened canines." Unless, of course, he were the rabid beast with sharpened canines in question. I have a few delicate places I wouldn't mind him taking a bite out of. The imagery alone makes me whimper, and my vagina is back on its knees begging to make this happen.

"Don't be sorry. Come here." He wraps his arms around my waist and gently slides me over until I'm sitting square between his legs. "I'll keep you safe."

My entire body goes rigid.

"It's okay," he whispers, pulling my shoulders into his chest until I slowly melt into him. His hand grazes my thigh, and a quick pulse of spasms go off deep inside me.

Oh God. I let out a tiny yelp as I break out in a rash of what can only be explained as spontaneous orgasms.

Crap, crap, crap! Stupid, *stupid* body.

"I hope you don't mind me holding you." He offers a dimpled grin, and my girl parts give a squeeze of approval.

"Plus, I can see you better this way." He rubs his cheek over the top of my head, and I twist in his arms to look up at him.

"Why do I get the feeling you're about to morph into the big bad wolf?" I lower my lashes as the words struggle from my throat. I'm far too close to him to be speaking, let alone breathing, and, God forbid, having multiple O's between his kneecaps. This is everything I've wanted, and, strangely, I'm more than afraid.

"I promise you I'm nothing like the big bad wolf." He rubs my back with his hand, and I gasp. "Hey, you're shaking." Bryson warms me with his oven-heated palms and creates enough friction to spark a thousand mini earthquakes between my legs. "I'll keep you toasty."

I give a shy smile. I don't dare confess that I'm not that cold—that I'm gloriously terrified as to where the night might lead—that my girl parts are just begging to extend an invitation for him to create friction elsewhere and *come* inside.

And, if the night leads in the right direction—he will.

"Back at the restaurant I asked you what you were afraid of." I let it hang there because he happened to follow that up with "me," and I'd like for him to expand on the concept. "Tell me what you're afraid, Bryson." I snuggle into his chest and look up at him as the moonbeams shine right through his prism-like eyes. I like it like this with Bryson. For the first time, it feels like we're a couple.

"It's nothing." He runs his tongue slowly over his bottom lip while staring off ahead at the steaming hot spring. "I guess at the end of the day I don't want to hurt anyone."

"Hurt anyone?" I pull back to examine him for a second. "You don't strike me as a monster."

"Yeah, well, the jury is still out on that one."

"I don't believe it for a second." I tweak his ribs, and he bucks into me with his lips curled.

"Whoa." Bryson tightens his fingers around my waist as a devilish grin takes over. "You just started a war, princess. You sure you want to go there?"

"Don't you dare!" My elbows crowd over my sides as I try to push his hands away. "I'm deathly ticklish, and I'll scream my head off if you even *think* about doing that."

"All right." A dull laugh brews in his chest. "I'll let you slide just this once. Be warned, you tickle me again, and it's on."

"You know what that sounds like?" I cock my head at him, teasing him as my hips nestle over his crotch.

"Like the threat is was?" He gives that cocky smile I've come to know and love.

"No, it sounded an awful lot like a dare. Like a double *dog* dare." I pinch his waist, and he jumps before running his fingers over my ribs then riding up just beneath my arms.

"*Okay!*" I scream through laughter. "You win!" I fall back onto the boulder, and he rolls on top of me, refining his torment technique.

"Say uncle." His head moves over mine as the heavens spray out behind him, and I always want to remember him this way—happy, with a crown of stars over his head.

"*Uncle!*"

"Say Bryson's the best." He slows his movements while I try to catch my breath.

"Bryson is the best." It gurgles from my throat with a screaming laugh. "You're great—I'm not." My hands track down low on his waist, and he catches me by the wrists.

"I think you're pretty great, Baya," he whispers just over my lips. His heated breath rakes over me like the blast from an oven, and I take his weight as he presses his body to mine. Our eyes lock with a magnetic pull. I pluck my hand free and touch the back of his neck, encouraging him to meet my lips.

"Baya," he whispers, closing his eyes momentarily. "Don't fall for me. I'm not worth it." A tragedy plays out over his features that I wish I could understand.

"I think you're more than worth it." I pant. "Do you think I'm worth it?" If he says no then I'll let this go, but there's something special between us, and if I can't deny it how can he?

"You're worth everything," he whispers, gently brushing the hair from my eyes. "It's me—I'm not worth the risk."

"Sometimes when you take a risk, great things happen—mountains move, and you see exactly what you've been waiting for, right there, in front of you." Hell, yes, I'm laying it on thick. "I think you're worth the risk, Bryson."

His breathing picks up. His heart thunders over my chest as if he were about to leap off a very tall building.

"I want you, Baya. I just don't know how we're going to do this."

My body convulses. Crap. This is a lousy time for my G spot to applaud his efforts.

"Let's start here." I pull him in, and Bryson crashes his lips to mine. His soft mouth tugs over me in an achingly slow manner. A moan gets caught in my throat, and a tingle rides between my thighs, exhilarating me all the way up to my belly button. My body quivers in a series of explosive waves, and I don't fight it. I'm not sure if it's possible to have an orgasm from simply being in his presence or if my hormones have chosen a heck of a bad time to short circuit, hell, I'm not sure I've ever had a proper orgasm due to the fact every other one was self-induced, but this feels otherworldly, magical in a damn illegal kind of way. Electrical currents are going off, neurons and synapsis are misfiring. An entire Fourth of July spectacular is happening in my body, and my girl parts are jumping up and down with elation—all because Bryson Edwards' hot mouth is over mine.

I give another groan and push him into me harder until he caves and blesses my mouth with his tongue in long, strong, lingering sweeps. Bryson moves his hands slowly up my arms until he's cradling my face in his hands, loving me with deep-throated kisses that I never want to end.

I run my hand up his shirt, and my fingers move over his rippling abs, nothing but skin over granite. I touch each of his grooves as his skin blisters over the pads of my fingers.

"Baya," he whispers, swiping his lips over mine. "We should talk about this—talk about us."

His eyes glow an eerie paper white as he lingers above me.

In the distance, the hot spring gurgles and hisses. It expels into the night with its slow dancing fog, curling its vapor-like fingers as it calls us over.

"You're right. I think we should talk about us." I glance to the hazy pool of water. "In there."

Bryson

The moon shines down over Baya with its white-hot spotlight. Her long hair shines like smoked glass, her face illuminates like an angel straight from the throne of God.

"You are so fucking beautiful." I outline her cheek with my finger.

I'm in. Screw Cole and his big brother shadow. Baya is going to have someone in her life one day, and I'd move heaven and earth for that someone to be me.

"Do you always throw a vulgarity in with your compliments?" She cinches her lips to the side, and I want to dive over her mouth again and never come out.

"Only when I can't control myself, and I am definitely having a hard time controlling myself around you." My chest rattles with a dull laugh because, holy shit, I've just fallen into Baya Brighton headfirst. I'm sunk, and I really don't care. What I'm feeling is real in every sense of the word. Love is on the horizon, and I don't really care who knows it at this point.

"Yeah?" She runs her finger up my chest and scratches at me lightly with her nails. For a second I imagine her running them over my back while she groans into my ear and makes all those sweet sounds I can't wait to hear from her. "I think you're cleverly trying to change the subject." She sits up and pulls off her sweater. "Last one in is a rotten egg!" She bounces to her feet and wriggles out of her signature cutoffs, but I'm enjoying the show too damn much to try and beat her.

What the hell. I tear off my shirt and kick off my shoes and socks, dropping my Levis as I bolt in front of her. I take her by the hand and help her down the embankment.

Baya laughs all the way over to the hot spring and dips her foot in.

She lets out a throaty groan while pulling her neck back, her eyes flutter with ecstasy, and, for a moment, I imagine me on top of her, exhibiting that exact same response.

"This feels amazing!" Her eyes roll back into her head, and I have to look away before my boner springs to life.

We sit down on the edge. I slip into the scalding water and hold out my hands to catch her. Baya's pale skin glows beneath her black lace bra, and it takes everything in me not to run my hands over her.

"Come in. I'll catch you."

Baya jumps into me without hesitating and locks her arms around my neck. She takes in a sharp breath as the water hugs her body. Her svelte hips land against my stomach, and I bite my lip in lieu of a groan.

"This feels like heaven." Her body relaxes over mine and her tits fall against my chest, heavy and weighted. The only thing that feels like heaven around here is Baya. "It's like God dropped a hot tub right here in the middle of nowhere," she muses.

"Really?" I pull her in toward the middle until her legs are no longer touching the sides. "Because I was just thinking it's like God dropped an angel off right here in the middle of nowhere, and I'm the lucky fool that caught her in my arms."

"Very funny." She averts her eyes at my cheesy pick up line.

"I meant every word."

Baya illuminates the night with her hundred-watt smile. She wraps her legs around my waist, and I lock off a groan in my throat as her flesh seals over mine.

"Angels, princesses..." She glances toward the top of the evergreens. "All references you might give your little sister." She leans in and takes a soft bite out of my lower lip.

I take in a smooth breath through my teeth.

"Trust me, Baya, the thoughts I'm having toward you are anything but brotherly. And you'll get to meet my little sister next weekend. She's no angel." The truth is, Annie is every bit a saint. "Okay, maybe she is, but that's beside the point." I sink us a little lower. "I think you're sexy as hell, Baya."

"That's better." She presses a kiss over my lips, and I can feel her fingers twitching behind her back. She plucks her bra off, tossing it onto the rocks while staring into me with the look of anticipation in her eyes.

"Baya." I ride my gaze, slowly down her features, her neck until I see her in all her God-given glory. "Damn, girl," I whisper, pulling her under just enough to cover her tits. "You're going to take me to the brink tonight."

"They missed you." She presses her bare chest into mine, and my hard-on rockets to life.

"I missed them, too." It takes everything in me to control my breathing.

"So are we all done talking?" She rides her hand up my thigh until she hits pay dirt, and I catch her. My dick and I are on the rails of temptation, and the train just lost its breaks.

"Not by a long shot." I slip my hands under her knees and hoist her high on my waist, safely away from my point of interest. "But I think we should do this"—I land a kiss over the nape of her neck and feel her sigh beneath me—"a lot."

Baya relaxes her head back as I graze my teeth over her flesh. I run my tongue up all the way to her ear and give a solid attempt to swallow her earlobe.

"Bryson," she gravels it out low, and my body electrifies in a series of pulsating waves. I've never felt this good, this alive with any other girl. Baya has the power to help me forget the past, erase it all together. This is strong, powerful, and I want to drink her down like an elixir, right here—right fucking now.

Her brother blinks through my mind, and I straighten. "Cole is going to blow my head off when he finds out." I pull back just enough to take in her beautiful face.

"Cole doesn't have to know—not at first anyway." Baya traces out an S over my chest, and I groan into her. "Besides, I like the thought of having you all to myself for a while." Her hand rides over my boxers, and this time I don't stop her. "I like the idea of having a delicious secret that only you and I know about."

I pull her hand up from over my balls and kiss it. "I'm falling for you, Baya." It feels safe like this to confess it with a midnight moon the only thing around to witness the event. I swore I'd never fall in love again, and here I am, hook, line, and sinker. Baya has me in ways she doesn't even know. "I want everything you're willing to give me."

Her eyes penetrate mine, serious, seductive like two emerald stones. "I've already fallen for you, Bryson—and I plan on giving you anything you want, anytime you want it." She dips her hands into the back of my boxers and gives my bare ass a squeeze. "I want to share every part of me with you." She runs her teeth over her bottom lip. "In the worst way."

"I want that, too." I firm my hands over her waist in an effort to keep them from wandering. "But I want to take it slow. I want your first time to be special." I press a warm kiss over her lips, and a branding iron of heat shoots through my body.

She pulls back. "I think *this* place is pretty darn special." A sweet laugh trembles from her. The water beading over her chest catches the light like a thousand falling stars. "But I'm okay with slow, too." She glances down at the water a moment. "I've never done anything like that before, so don't expect much from me."

"I wouldn't worry." I spin us in a slow circle. "You've already got everything I'm dying for, Baya. Swear to God, I've never wanted anyone like I'm wanting you." It's my turn to drop my gaze to the water. I look back up and pull her in by the chin with my finger. "I swear to you—I won't break your heart. I'm committed to loving you exactly how you deserve."

Tears bloom in her eyes, and it's the last thing I expect.

"Whoa, did I say something wrong?" I pull us out of the water a few inches and let the night air cool us off.

"No"—she shakes her head, wiping away the tears—"you said everything right." She tilts her head back, taking in a deep breath before reverting her gaze to mine. "I hope you don't think this is creepy, but nobody has ever cared for me the way you do—at least not since my dad passed away." She shrugs. "My mom was busy trying to keep a roof over our heads, and Cole was busy telling me who to be and how to act. But you"—she pulls her lips into a sad smile—"you're so positive. You make me feel safe. I love that about you. And—I think I'm falling in love with you." The smile glides off her face. Her legs go slack around my waist, and I pull them up again.

"I think I'm falling in love with you, too. In fact, I know I am." I press in until our mouths fuse in one eternal kiss. Baya dances her tongue over mine, lounges in my mouth as if she's setting up shop and plans on staying for years, and I hope to God she is.

Baya says she's never done anything, and I'm damn glad. I want to teach her everything, be right there while she's experiencing the zenith of pleasure with my body buried deep inside her.

I ride my hands up over her waist and round out the front until my thumbs press over her nipples. She's so fucking soft, I'm about to lose it. But I don't. I want to save everything and wait for that perfect moment with Baya. I want to love her until the morning, and then that won't be enough. Whenever it is, I hope it's soon. I don't think I can hold out much longer.

§

The week melts by like snow in springtime.

Baya and I take the bikes out each morning before class and ride up to the Witch's Cauldron to steal a moment—safe away from Cole and the long line of sorority girls he has swarming his bedroom night after night.

I told Holt I was bringing Baya home this weekend, asked him to man the fort at the Black Bear while I was gone. I haven't told Mom or Annie yet, I thought I'd spring her on them sort of the way the universe sprang her on me. Baya's been the best surprise—the biggest relief.

The last thing I need to do on Friday, before I officially steal Baya away for the weekend, is work my ass off at Capwell Inc. for a few hours. The founder's grandson, Ryder, and I share an office. He's a grad student at Briggs, along with his cousin Aubree, the curator of my misery here at the Capwell advertising division.

"Anything new with you and Ms. Sawyer?" I ask, pushing the daunting stack of paper the hell away from me for a moment. It's no secret Ryder still pines for Laney. They had a head on collision of a break up last winter after years of waiting to be together, and now it's like they're virtual strangers.

He shakes his head just barely. You can see the hurt swelling up in his eyes, so I don't push it, hell I feel bad for bringing it up to begin with.

"She ever mention me?" He swallows hard while studying my face for clues.

Laney hasn't let his name escape her lips since Christmas, but I'll be the last to tell him.

"Probably." I pull the files back and sift through them. "I'm not around her much."

This is where relationships get tricky, the messy breakup that leaves you jonesing for clues while trying to piece together what the hell might have happened.

Aubree breezes in the room and zaps the energy right out of it. I've already tweaked the files she slung in my direction this morning. She's just a grad student, but something tells me in about five years she'll be running this place.

"Doing anything fun this weekend?" Aubree dips her cleavage in my face while landing a fresh stack of files over my desk. I glance back at Ryder for help, but he's conveniently buried his face in his laptop.

"Just going away." I pull back until she clears the air space. Her perfume hangs in the air like a toxic cloud, and my eyes start to water.

"All by your lonesome or you bringing someone special?" She slips her finger in her mouth and pulls it out slow, like a promise. Her hair glows orange under the harsh lights, and her makeup is set in a thick purple line over her upper lids like long, dark wings that are about to take flight.

"My girlfriend's coming." Did that just fly out of my mouth?

Both Aubree and Ryder widen their eyes. They knew Steph. They know how it all went down and why.

I freeze with a file in my hand, my eyes locked over the desk as if something blasphemous just flew from my lips. I hadn't had an official girlfriend since way back when with Steph, and an ice bath floods through my veins. I promised I wouldn't go there again, and yet I did. Sometimes the stupidest promises are the ones we make to ourselves. But I'm damn glad that's one I broke. Baya is worth breaking a thousand rules for.

"Girlfriend?" She clutches at her throat. A devilish smile twitches on her lips as if I'm about to inundate her with the gossip of my love life. "So? Who's the lucky little tramp this week? Please, dish."

"Baya Brighton." I don't hesitate this time. "She's no tramp, and, I can promise you, this is going to last much longer than a week." A weight lifts from me just getting Baya's name out there, and as my girlfriend no less. It feels as though I've lanced a wound. My entire body sighs with relief. I'm not too sure I care if Cole is let in on our secret either. I plan on being with Baya a long, long time—forever, if she'll have me. Sometimes when you find the right person, you just know. And I've definitely found the right person in Baya.

"Baya Brighton?" She scratches at her neck while scanning the ceiling. "Why does that sound familiar?"

"She tried to rush for Alpha Chi, and you kicked her out." I flop the files back down on the desk and relax in my seat.

"Oh, *that* Baya Brighton...right." Her eyes enlarge like twin pools of fire. Aubree Vincent is the devil in disguise, and half the time she doesn't bother to disguise it. "She's a spicy little bitch. But then you've always liked them a little on the wild side."

"Be nice." I fold my arms across my chest. "Oddly, she still wants in after meeting you." I shake my head at the thought. "Go figure."

"Really?" Aubree appears equally amused. "Well"—she exhales hard—"if she wants in that bad, I'll give her another chance. But I'd have to pull her under my wing. Rush is over for the most part."

"You'd do that for me? I hear breaking sorority rules, especially when it comes to rushing new pledges, is the equivalent of committing thirty different felonies." The Greeks have a tight government. It makes Washington look like a bunch of pussies.

"It's more like fifty." She slides over my desk just inches from my chest and runs her finger the length of my jaw. "And, of course, I'd do that." Aubree leans in until her tits try to sway their way out of that sling of a shirt she's got on. "I'd do just about anything for you." She gives a little wink. "Why do you think you're sitting in that chair?"

A beat of silence drifts by. I've always wondered how I won out half the class at the Whitney Briggs School of Business to land in this treasured spot, and now I know. Figures. I shoot Ryder a look, and he shakes his head into his laptop.

Aubree purrs. "I loved you the moment I laid eyes on you, Bryson Edwards," she says it serious as shit, and, for a moment, I believe her. Her features harden as she takes me in. "But you never seem to fall for any of my tricks, do you?" She runs her hand down my chest, and I catch her. She plucks it back and bounces off the desk as if the entire exchange never took place. "Baya Brighton," she purrs. "Girlfriend, huh?" She leers at me as she walks out the door. "We'll see how long that lasts." She gives a cackle that echoes down the hall.

Ryder lifts his chin, a wry smile embedded in his face. "You know she's going to make your girlfriend's life a living hell."

"She won't. Aubree's all bark and no bite." Not that her ten-foot lady-boner didn't go unnoticed just now. Hopefully she'll pole vault her way to friendlier pastures with that thing. The last place she'll find some satisfaction is with me. I'm all Baya's from here on out.

He shakes his head. "And here I thought you knew her well. She'll bite your balls off and, trust me, the only one barking will be you. You'd better watch your back around her—and your little girlfriend, too." He twitches his brows before scooping up his laptop and heading out the door.

There's no way I'd let anyone hurt Baya, least of all me. Years have passed since high school, and I finally know how to treat a girl. And I'm determined to treat her well.

Please, God, don't let me hurt Baya.

I couldn't live with myself if I did.

❧✥❧

Early that evening, while I zip up my duffle bag, Cole stumbles in and drops his backpack to the floor, heavy as bricks.

"Where you off to?" He belches as he makes his way to the fridge and plucks out a beer.

"Picking up Annie and taking her home. I thought I'd help my mom out around the house while I'm there. I'll be back late Sunday. Don't wait up for me, sweet cheeks." I give a little wink in his direction.

"Don't worry, I won't." He salutes me with his beer.

"Hit the Black Bear for me," I say, taking a seat at the bar across from him. "Keep an eye on my brother—make sure he doesn't do anything goofy like run off with the safe."

"Will do." He nods, caging me in with a hard stare. "Have you been keeping an eye on my sister?" Cole tilts into me while those ditches in his face invert with disapproval.

Fuck. I've been minding my P's and Q's around her as best as I can, and, as much credit as I give Aubree for being the wicked witch of the East, I don't think this is her doing either.

"Your sister?" I ask like I've no clue who the hell she might be. "What are you taking about?" I snatch up a near empty water bottle and down it.

"Just wondered if you noticed the way she's been looking at you." He blows out a breath of relief and scratches at the back of his neck. "I've got to set her up with some nice kid. I know she's got hormones, but I'm scared shitless she's going to knock on all the wrong doors, you know what I mean?" His eyes drill into mine, and, for the first time, I see desperation in them. "It's like all of a sudden she's all hopped up. Just do me a favor, man"—Cole leans in with an earnestness I've never seen in him before—"if she shows any interest, just turn her down flat. She's not another notch on the wall." He's practically pleading with me. "I wouldn't do that to your sister, dude. I would hope to God you wouldn't do that to mine."

The thought of someone turning Annie into a notch sets my blood to an instant boil. But that would never happen to Annie, she's too sweet—and so is Baya. The last thing I'm going to do is log our encounter like some barbaric conquest. She means everything to me, and I plan on showing her just that. At least up until her brother knifes my balls off.

"There's no way in hell I'd turn her into a notch, dude."

Nope. I plan on loving Baya in ways like I've never loved anyone, and there aren't enough walls in the world to keep a record of the ways I plan on loving her.

The only notch Baya Brighton is carving is the one over my heart.

5

When it Happens

Baya

Fall breaks out in a spectacular show of glory over Whitney Briggs University. It brings all of the wonder and drama it can afford as it slowly turns the campus into an auburn-colored wonderland. Leaves in every shade of gold, brown, russet, fawn, and jade decorate the walkways, but my favorite are the ones that look as though they've been smeared with lovers blood. The indelible stain of a secret covenant made between two people who've sworn to belong to one another forever. That's what I'm hoping will happen this weekend. Not the actual slitting of the wrists and mashing of bloodlines. I'm just hoping for a good old fashion love story to write itself across the night sky in shooting orgasmic stars. Actually, I'm sort of hoping for multiple cosmic events to occur and in rather quick succession. I envision Bryson lying over me, pouring a fire into my mouth by way of his—that rock hard body pressing into mine until we're weak with passion, aching for more, just satisfying the hunger we have for one another in one long fornicating loop that puts all of Jeanie Waters collective efforts to shame. I've never made love to anyone before, I've never had any kind of sex whatsoever, heck, I don't even have a hand job under my belt, but, nevertheless, I know it'll be incredible because I'll have Bryson right there with me—*in* me. And it all seems far too incredible to imagine.

"Brighton!" A female voice calls from behind as I lug my weekend bag with me across campus. Bryson thought it'd be a good idea if we left separately, so I've been roaming aimlessly since this afternoon, familiarizing myself with the nooks and crannies of Whitney Briggs only to find they already house warm bodies, and the last thing those warm bodies are doing in those nooks and crannies is studying for midterms. It's as if all of Whitney Briggs has caught Jeanie's fornicating fever. Honest to God, someone should call the HAZMAT team to contain the syphilis outbreak before it reaches epidemic proportions and storms the world as the new killer plague. It would figure that Jeanie Waters' crotch has the potential to unleash cataclysmic atrocities on all mankind.

Laney waves me over to the outdoor patio at Hallowed Grounds, and I head in that direction. Roxy is with her, and they've got a plethora of textbooks and notebooks spread out over the table, implying that actual studying might be taking place. Obviously its crunch time, but, technically, midterms aren't for another two weeks, so I refuse to be intimidated by their scholastic show of bravado. Why sweat it when I can sweat with Bryson? I say screw Whitney Briggs, and I'll screw Bryson Edwards, too. A million lousy jokes have been waging an assault on my frontal lobe all afternoon because, face it, I'm about to have my V-card revoked, and I'm scared spitless. Sarcasm has always helped me cope when life throws me a couple of hairy curve balls, and if stupid shit racking my brain helps me through the ordeal then I say bring it and its long, hard, one-eyed bat, too. Besides, sex with Bryson is in the bounds, and it's all I can do to keep a pornographic bubble from forming over the top of my head for the entire world to see. I feel transparent, naked in a crowd of thousands—the virgin who's about to *go all the way*, shaking in her proverbial FMs. It's not at all what I envisioned this time in my life would be like.

"What's up, chica?" Laney pulls out a seat for me, and I plop down between them. "You on tonight?"

"No, but I'll be hanging with the boss does that count?" I bite down on my lip and watch as their faces ignite like street lamps. Clearly we've treaded into the red-light district, so already I know where this conversation is headed.

They break out in a choir of *oohs,* and I blush at the thought of what might happen tonight.

"Someone at this table dated her b-o-s-s once." Roxy glances at Laney, and they have a mini standoff complete with a silent argument.

"Did you date Bryson?" My hand flies to my chest in horror. I like Laney and the last thing I want to do is

149

imagine her naked while wrestling with my boyfriend. *Boyfriend.* I swoon into the idea.

"No!" She shakes her head, and her dark hair whips around in the wind. "Not *that* boss—another boss. It turns out he wasn't really my anything." She lowers her gaze to the table.

"It was my brother," Roxy offers. "And it ended badly." She says that last part so low I hardly heard it. "So where's the big date?" Roxy bears into me, changing the subject rather efficiently.

"It's sort of a weekend thing." I shrug. "He's taking me to his house."

"Shut up." Laney straightens. Her mouth falls open as if I'd just announced we were planning to elope.

"*Yes.*" I nod incredulously. "He was going home, and he just sort of invited me to come along. Plus, this way, we can keep things under the radar just a little bit longer." I filled them in earlier in the week about our plan to keep Cole in the dark until we're ready. Bryson is still convinced he won't see the next day once we tell him. Of course, he's right. In fact, if Cole finds out, my newfound boyfriend is as good as dead. Cole is pretty focused on keeping my virginity intact for the next fifty years or so, never mind the fact he's nothing more than a human dildo to the female population of Whitney Briggs. I bet all the sorority girls say, *why bother with batteries when you can bed Cole Brighton? He's the Eveready penis!*

"So where does your brother think you're going?" Roxy gives a coy smile as if she were proud of my dubious endeavor.

"Pluto," I tease. "A.k.a.—*book* camp." I shake my head at the literary lunacy of it all. "It was all I could think of that he might remotely approve of. Little does he know my book boyfriend just morphed into the real deal, and his name happens to be Bryson Orgasm-on-Demand Edwards."

The two of them break out in cackles.

"*Book* camp!" Roxy sighs. "Is there such a thing?"

"No clue. But, if there's not, there should be. It sounds like a great cover for just about any story—get it? Story?" They groan in unison.

"Baya"—Laney leans in—"Bryson is taking you to his house, to meet his *family*. This is really a big step for him." Her pale skin glows against the backdrop of the late afternoon. It's been getting dark so early. It feels like midnight by four o'clock. It's exhausting and hauntingly erotic all at the same time.

"It's a big step for me, too." Not that I'll be volunteering to haul him to Texas anytime soon. I'm pretty sure Mom would string him up by the balls if he even looked at me in a sexual manner. "I mean we'll be with his family, so it'll practically be a platonic weekend."

"Platonic? I'm pretty sure that's not in his lexicon. So—what *are* the sleeping arrangements, anyway?" Roxy narrows in on me as she cuts to the nocturnal chase.

Sleeping arrangements? That sweet spot between my thighs spasms at the thought of sleeping under the same roof, let alone the same *bed,* as Bryson. I wonder if one can have too many orgasms, and how exactly I might explain this to the ER staff once I can't stop convulsing with pleasure.

"Like I said, his mom will be there, so we'll probably sleep in separate rooms. I'll probably crash on the couch. God knows I'm used to it." *God* what if she's one of those liberal moms who totally roots for her kids to hook up under her roof? What if she's out right now buying candles and specialty condoms that light up just to make the occasion oh so special? I shake the thought out of my head. My mother would be stocking up on pepper spray and stun guns—a rape whistle and a club.

"When there's a hard-on, there's a way." Laney nods into her hormonal theory. "He wants you." She takes a sip of her drink. "*Bad.*"

"So have you done it yet?" Roxy crinkles her nose as she awaits my salacious response.

"No, we haven't done *it,* so I'm pretty sure our first time won't be with his mom in the next room listening to the headboard rattle. That's one of the reasons I'm dying to get away from Cole's apartment. I'm so sick of listening to him wallop his trollops night after night. You'd think the neighbors would have called the swat team by now the way it sounds like machine gun fire is exploding from his bedroom. It's like a hostage situation in there or a really loud marathon of Scar Face going on, but the only one getting scarred around there is me—*emotionally.*"

Laney spits her coffee just past my shoulder.

"Sorry!" She gags out a laugh. "It's just that the visual was too amusing." She sops up the mess she made. "I've been to the Edwards house—more like estate." She lowers her lashes at me. "It's pretty big. There are an awful lot of places and spaces someone could run off to if they wanted. Are you scared?"

"Why would she be scared?" Roxy sticks her pen between her teeth a moment. "Oh my, God—you're a virgin!"

"Shh!" I bounce a few inches in my seat. "No need to pull out the mega phone. It's not a big deal. I was just waiting for the right person, that's all." I give a shy smile. "And, lucky me, because I found him."

"*Aww!*" They sing in unison.

"Baya!" A male voice booms across the courtyard, and Bryson waves with that ridiculously gorgeous smile. My girl parts and I sigh in unison.

"That's my ride." I pull my bag up over my shoulder. "Any quick tips?" My heart races at the prospect of what might happen this weekend—hell, right now in his truck if he wanted.

Roxy shakes her head. "Just be yourself and have fun. I promise, it'll come naturally." She winks. "And, if you're lucky, so will you."

If I'm lucky. My girl parts clench in a mini rebellion. I'm always lucky with Bryson Edwards around.

Laney leans in, she cuts her gaze over at Bryson, and a sorrowful look crosses her face. "That boy needs some TLC. Just love him sweetly."

Love him sweetly. That's exactly what I plan on doing.

෨෬

Bryson and I drive down the city streets of Hollow Brook as the leaves rain over the sidewalks like buckets full of rustic-colored confetti. An entire army of gardeners attack the rolling green lawn in front of the public library. I watch as their weed whackers get close to the border garden filled with marigolds—their proud orange poms shiver in fear of decapitation.

Bryson swings into a parking lot and only after the fact do I read the sign on the side of the building in front of us, *Quincy Howard School for the Deaf and Hard of Hearing.*

"I wondered how far we'd get before you pulled over to steal a kiss." I unbuckle my seatbelt and slide into him.

A naughty smile twitches on his lips. "Come here." Bryson pulls me in, and our mouths find one another, desperately hungry for more than we could ever hope to accomplish sitting in the front seat of his supped-up monster truck. Bryson plunges his tongue in my mouth and teases me with laboriously slow, agonizingly sweet kisses. A moan vibrates from his throat to the most intimate part of me, and it quivers with an erotic approval. "Baya," he pulls back and takes me in. "You're amazing, you know that?" he whispers in awe as if seeing me for the very first time.

"*You're* amazing." I take in his features and memorize them. His brows pitch, annunciating the barely-there scar just under his left eye. "What happened?" I touch it carefully as if the wound had never healed.

"Fell off a horse and hit a pipe sticking up from the ground. I'm pretty lucky I didn't lose an eye that day."

"That's scary." I run my fingers through his thick hair. "I'm glad you didn't hurt your beautiful eyes." I press in another kiss, and my lips linger soft as clouds over him. "You make every moment special whether we're together or not. But I *much* prefer when we're together." Our lips meet again, and this time it's fueled with lust that only the prospect of sharing something so incredible might bring. My body aches to have him. It's as if he's pouring his lust for me straight down my throat, and I'm drinking it to the dregs like the most maddening wine. I'm drunk off Bryson Edwards, addicted in the very best way.

"We'll be together all weekend." He pulls back. The trace of a smile never leaves his lips.

A harsh knock explodes over the passenger's side window, and I jump back to find a sandy-haired blonde waving at us. She's pretty with familiar, clear blue eyes.

"God, you attract them everywhere you go. Who's that?" My stomach sinks at the sight of her. She's so beautiful I'm almost afraid to ask.

"That"—he unlocks the truck, and she opens the back door—"is my sister, Annie." His fingers start contorting in a strange formation, and it takes a second for me to register he's signing to her.

Annie waves at me, and her smile widens. She signs something over to Bryson before latching the seatbelt over her waist.

"She says she's happy to meet you. She also said you're far too pretty for me." He frowns over at her. "And I happen to agree." He starts up the truck, and we're on our way again.

"It's nice to meet you, too," I say as we head back out onto the highway.

"Annie was born completely deaf," he says, glancing back at her in the rearview mirror. "She's pretty good at reading lips most of the time, unless, of course, you sign. Then she understands you perfectly."

"God," I whisper. "I'm sorry." I sink in my seat a little. "I had no idea. She's so beautiful."

"She's a trooper. Annie doesn't consider it a curse. To her it's a blessing. She likes the kids she goes to school with. Annie's an encourager. She likes to build people up when they get down."

"What grade is she in?" I feel horrible talking about her when she's less than two feet from us.

"Senior. She's filling out her app for Whitney Briggs in the fall. They have accommodations that can help her out with classes, so I feel pretty good about it." He gives a thumbs up to the backseat, and Annie reciprocates.

My heart melts watching Bryson interact with his sister. Somehow meeting Annie only makes my heart expand for him even more. And here I thought it was full. Bryson keeps surprising me in ways I could never imagine. I love everything about him, and, now, I can't wait to show him in the most intimate way.

We drive about a half hour until the cityscape is traded for expansive properties with long bridle fences that stretch acre after acre. Horses dot the countryside, Arabians, palominos, paints. I've seen my fair share of horses after moving to Texas. I miss seeing their regal beauty, and it hasn't been two months.

The houses expand around us in both girth and width, each with an entire row of three and four car garages tucked beneath them. We drift into a ritzy neighborhood lined with luxury SUVs and newly minted sports cars, and I can't help but marvel. After my dad passed away, there never seemed to be enough of anything, friends and family included.

Bryson pulls up to a large wrought iron fence and punches in a code at the entry before the gates part like wings, and we drive on through. A small winding road takes us past a series of juniper trees before revealing an enormous stone structure far too big to ever be the home of just one family.

My mouth opens as if to ask the question.

"This is Mom's house," Bryson says as he parks close to the stairs that lead up to a grand entrance. "My dad paid most of it off as a parting gift."

"It's amazing," I whisper, taking in the Spanish style abode. The arched windows, the rounded curves of the towers that stretch on either side of it, give it a fairytale appeal.

We get out, and Bryson comes over and picks up my bag in one hand, my hand in the other, and my adrenaline soars. He's never held my hand on campus, and for sure not at the apartment, but here we were free to do anything we want.

Annie skips up the stairs ahead of us and bursts through the front door.

The house looks like it belongs in another country, another time, another *world*. Bryson hoists our bags over his shoulder and leads me up the steps.

"I can't wait for you to meet my mom. She's going to love you."

"She is?" Suddenly the idea of meeting his mother has me shaking in my impractically high heels. I've never met a boy's mother before, especially not when I'm spending the night, and her son is setting an inferno off in the most intimate part of me just from the simple act of holding my hand. I try to call off my rabid vagina, but it's too late. She's bucking and reeling from being so close to Bryson—to his *bedroom*. "Does she know I'm coming?"

3:AM KISSES

Unfortunately that can be taken both literally and figuratively.

"Nope." He gives my hand a squeeze. "I wanted it to be a surprise."

Crap. Not all surprises are good, but secretly I'm hoping I'm a good one.

"You'll do fine." He brings my hand to his mouth and kisses it. "Besides, I'm dying to show you off."

Just hearing that sets the butterflies off in my stomach.

Bryson leads us in through the glass double doors where Annie and a tall woman with a bob haircut and large black-rimmed glasses greets us. A black lab, just like my own, runs circles around me, and I bend over and scratch behind his ears while he licks me silly.

"Easy, Nitro." Bryson gives him a pat on the head, and the panting pooch retreats.

His mother steps in. "Well who is this beautiful young lady?" Her eyes expand, clear as a summer sky, just like Bryson's.

"Mom, this is Baya. Baya—this is my mom, Miranda."

"It's nice to meet you." I reach over and shake her hand briefly.

An awkward moment of silence thumps by, and both she and Annie take their time to inspect me from head to toe. Nitro lets out a little bark and breaks the ice.

"Would you look at how gorgeous you are?" His mother crimps her lips. "I bet you're illegal in twelve different states."

My entire body flushes with heat as I cut a look to Bryson. I hardly believe my face is criminal, but I appreciate her effort.

"It's actually all fifty." Bryson reels me in by the waist. "So I might need to help her hide out for a while." He pulls me in closer until I relax over his body. "If you don't mind, I'm going to give her the tour and get us settled in."

Annie signs over to him, and he nods.

Bryson leans into me. "She's got a friend spending the night and asked if we wanted to watch a movie with them later."

I nod into him. "I love you," it speeds out of me. Crap. "I mean, I'd love to."

But it's too late. The giggle fest has begun as everyone around me chortles at my verbal mishap, laden with hearts and arrows, and, well, the truth.

"I'm glad." His mother smiles. "But no movie before dinner," she chides to her daughter. "Meet me in the dining room in half an hour." She looks to us all. "I've got a roasted duck and a gumbo I've been working on all day."

Annie makes a face.

"Don't worry," Bryson whispers into me. "I've got plans for dessert." He gives my ribs a tweak. "Baya and I will whip up some cookies."

"Nice," it purrs out of me. For a moment I thought he was propositioning me in front of his family.

"Race you up the steps," he says, taking off for the sweeping staircase.

I bolt around him and barely crest the top a second before he does, with Nitro hot on my heels.

"I win," I pant.

"It's a tie." He presses a kiss over my lips. "Plus, I had forty pounds of luggage." He bumps the bags over his shoulders as Nitro hightails it back downstairs. "What do you have in here anyway? The bricks of technology?"

"Actually"—I step into his chest as he pants into me—"I left my laptop behind this weekend. I didn't think I'd get much studying done with you around." I glance down at the floral carpet that bleeds into the hall. "I thought maybe we could do other things." I wanted to add, now that my brother isn't haunting us with his vagina protection shield, but I'd rather leave all mention of Cole and missile-defense systems outside these walls for the weekend.

Bryson pulls me in. His hands warm my waist before riding low over my bottom, and my body whimpers into him.

"I was sort of hoping we'd do other things, too." He gives a smile that borders on wicked. "I hope this weekend is everything you want it to be."

Dear God. "It already is."

Bryson offers a kiss that lingers this time. His supple lips smooth over mine and rain that special fire only he can produce right down into my soul.

A pair of footsteps come up on us quick, and we part ways quickly only to find Annie clicking her tongue at us before rushing back downstairs.

"Annie's room." He nods to the door at the end of the hall. "Holt's," he touches a door as we head in the opposite direction. "Your room." He opens the door quiet as a whisper then nods at the room next door. "That's mine."

"Oh"—a flood of relief fills me that he's practically within reach—"thank you." My face heats up for no good reason. "So"—I lean into the doorframe—"is this where you stash all the girls you bring home for the weekend?" I don't know why I went there. I guess, deep down, a part of me wants to know just how many girls his mother might find illegal.

"I guess so." Bryson takes in a breath as he settles my bag on the floor. His eyes float back to mine, serious, tender with their gaze. "I've never brought a girl home before, so, in a way, I'm setting a precedent with you."

My heart thumps its way into my throat. My ears pulsate with a rhythm all their own.

Bryson Edwards has never brought a girl home before, and now that girl is me.

"I don't know what to say," I whisper as he comes in close, his breath feathering over my cheek.

"Say this." Bryson covers my mouth with his, and we indulge in a heated exchange right there in the doorway that just so happens to be unblemished with tally marks, real or imagined. His tongue roams over mine, his teeth bite over my lip playfully. I don't stand a chance this weekend. I'm already his in every single way.

Bryson tracks his hands up my thigh and stops shy of my bottom. I reach down and pull him up a few inches until he's cupping my curves in his hands, and a slight laugh gurgles from his throat to mine.

"This is just the beginning." I whisper right into his mouth.

Bryson strings a trail of kisses up my neck and gives a gentle bite over my ear.

"A beautiful beginning," he whispers, and every cell in me sings the body electric.

This weekend is starting to feel like the beginning of the rest of my life.

And with Bryson by my side, it will be more than beautiful.

Bryson

I give Baya a tour of the house, the most important room being my bedroom. She walks slowly around the periphery looking at the trophies on my bookshelf, the lack of actual *books*, which I'm sure she finds unimpressive. She runs her hand over the felt pendant that reads *Whitney Briggs,* and I don't bother telling her that my mom put that up while I was away my first semester. Baya pauses at something over my desk and lingers.

"Who's this girl?" It comes out so innocent, it doesn't even faze me at first.

I bounce off the bed in a single bound and make my way over.

Fuck.

I flip the picture down and take a step back as if I just put out a grass fire. I don't know what I was thinking. I knew that picture was here, and it's like it didn't even register. I should get rid of it. God knows it's burned itself into my mind. It's the one of me and Steph locked in an embrace, floating on the lake in a canoe like we had the rest of our lives ahead of us to do just that. It's when things were still good. I guess everything is good when you're both still alive.

"Whoa." Baya holds up her hands as if she were about to get arrested. "So that's the hot spot." She bites down over her lip. "You want to talk about it?" Her forehead wrinkles, and, for a second, I think she might cry—that we both might.

"I'm sorry." I pull her in by the waist and touch her forehead to mine. "I'm not ready to go there." I'm not sure I ever will be. "One day." One day seems like a good answer. It hurts too much to think about. And, now, I have Baya—her whole heart, and it feels unfair to everyone involved. It was easier when it was girls by the dozen falling into my bed. I could put my heart in a bottle and toss it into the ocean, forget about it forever if I wanted. But Baya plucked the bottle right out of the sea. She's holding it there in her sweet hand, tenderly, carefully. And now we're both staring down at my barely-beating heart wondering what the hell's the matter with it.

Baya pulls me in and melts her lips over mine. She offers slow, lingering kisses that scrape the pain out of the deepest part of me—that have the ability to cleanse my mortal soul. Baya should store her affection and sell it as a balm. She's the light at the end of this very dark tunnel. And, if she keeps leading me by the heartstrings, I think I might make it out alive.

"Maybe we should go down to dinner," I whisper. I'm hoping that will brush the patina of grief off this night. I'm ready to galvanize my relationship with Baya, and the last thing I want to do is focus on the tragedy in my life.

"Dinner sounds great."

She'll change her mind once she tries Mom's cooking, but I'll let her decipher that for herself.

Downstairs, Mom and Annie have already set the table, so we take our seats. Nitro sits dutifully next to Baya and me, and, I'm sure between the two of us, he'll score more of Mom's questionable food than he'll want. Mom dishes out the gumbo, and I watch as Baya eyes the concoction as if an alligator might pop out—and, knowing Mom, it might.

"So"—Mom steadies her eyes over Baya with that peace about her that I was hoping for—"Bryson mentioned you were from Texas. What made you choose Whitney Briggs?"

"My dad." She glances over at me and gives a sad smile. "He went there. My brother and I both wanted to attend, especially after he passed away." She pauses a second, and my heart breaks for her. "He was struck by a drunk driver while he was on his bike. He was a cyclist. He loved to ride."

I don't remember her mentioning a drunk driver—and here I have her working at a fucking bar. Crap.

"I'm so sorry." Mom touches her hand to her lips. Annie looks equally distraught, so I don't bother translating. "Bryson has had nothing but nice things to say about your brother. I'd love to meet him one day. He's been rather an enigma these past few years. Maybe he can come with you next time?"

Baya shifts uncomfortably in her seat. Mom doesn't realize that if we brought Cole, bulletproof vests might be necessary—for me anyway.

"I think that would be great." Baya's lips rubber band into the world's quickest smile. "You have a beautiful home." She looks from Mom to Annie.

And, so it goes, with the on again off again, awkward dinner conversation until finally Annie offers to clear the dishes.

"Baya"—Mom folds her hands where her plate once sat—"tell me how you and Bryson met."

Shit.

I blink a smile over at Baya, and my gaze dips to her chest a moment. Her perfect tits were the ultimate hello, but I'll be the last to admit it to my mother.

"I..." Her teeth graze her lips. Baya is cute as hell when she's in hot water. "I was struggling with my luggage and he offered to help."

Well done. I raise my brows at her. And points for telling the truth.

"What a gentleman." Mom swoons into the idea. "That's my Bry, Bry..."

And it's a wrap.

I push my seat out. "Baya, you want to help with dessert?"

"Yes." She hops up so fast, you'd think her feet were on springs.

Baya and I make our way to the kitchen where Annie already has the dishwasher running.

Annie signs over to me. *You found a good one. I'm proud of you.* She wraps her arms around me for a brief

167

second. *You deserve to be happy, even though I know you don't think so.*

I give her a firm hug before she waves at Baya and leaves the room.

"I like your sister." Baya pulls me in by the belt loop. Her perfume swoops around me like a vanilla whisper.

"She likes you, too. So does my mom."

"So I got the seal of approval?" She dips her chin just enough to let me know she's flirting.

"It doesn't really matter what they think." I dot a kiss on the tip of her nose. "I'd love you anyway."

There it is again, that L word. I'm not so sure she's comfortable with me using it so liberally, but I can't help it. I'm in so fucking deep, I can't see straight. I'm head over heels—all of my sanity has left the building. My lips find their way to hers, and Baya grazes over my tongue with her teeth. My hands glide up her sweater and round out over her hips. I love touching Baya this way. Having the freedom to do so without thinking Cole might lodge a hatchet in my skull from behind.

A loud clatter erupts, and we both jump.

"Sorry!" Mom freezes, doing her best impersonation of a deer in the headlights. "I was just passing through and dropped this." She holds up an aluminum tray.

"We were just about to bake cookies," Baya says it so fast, it sounds like the excuse it is.

"Not a problem. I'm off to bed. Goodnight!" Mom zips out of the kitchen so quick you'd think she saw a ghost.

"That wasn't awkward." Baya's dimples press in as she frowns.

"Well, I'd hate for you to be a liar. It looks like we'd better do some baking." I wrap my arms back around her waist. "Hey"—I pull her in as the smile melts from my face—"I don't remember you telling me the details about your dad." The truth is I hardly have the guts to go there.

She lowers her lashes and blows a breath over my chest. "That's exactly what happened."

"Is that why you don't drink?"

"Only partially." She shrinks a little. "Is that lame? I really don't care for the smell, so I assume the taste is not far off."

"No, it's not lame. There's nothing lame about you. Does it bother you to work at the bar?"

She shakes her head. "In fact, I always offer to call a cab for someone before they take off, and twice already I've been taken up on it. It feels good to know that I might be averting another tragedy." She shrugs. "Is that silly?"

"That's damn right heroic." I land a careful kiss over her lips. "How about we implement a program where we make it routine to ask if anyone needs a cab?"

"That would be great."

"What was your dad's name?" I wince when I say the word, *was*.

"Charlie."

"We can call it Charlie's Plan."

"You'd do that?"

"*Yes.*" I brush her hair from her eyes. "Hell, yes."

169

"And"—she gives a coy smile—"if they're really ripped and refuse our offer, we can implement the *Sorry Charlie* program and take away their keys."

"Sounds like a master plan. I'll get that going at all three sites." I pull her in and rock her slowly while dropping a kiss to the top of her head. "Now, let's bake some cookies, girl."

Baya and I tag-team the kitchen, preheating the oven and one another the way we keep stealing kisses. Baya is hotter than a firecracker the way she holds the spatula, the way she dips her finger into the side of the bowl and licks it clean.

I can feel my hard-on begging to tick to life, and it's taking all of my self-control not to bend her over the counter and take her like I want. That's not entirely true, I'd like to make love to her, slow and easy, all night if she'd let me, even though hot-counter sex is pretty high on the list.

The timer goes off, and Baya pulls out the first batch.

"Smells like heaven." She closes her eyes while hovering above them. She looks lost in ecstasy, her lips parting as if they're begging for just one bite.

I'm ready to fall into the heaven that is Baya Brighton, and I'm hoping she's ready, too.

৪৩

After a small eternity of feeding each other chocolate chips by way of our teeth, we bring a batch of cookies over to Annie and her friend. They're sitting on the floor in a pile of pillows, so Baya and I opt for the couch, and settle in to watch the movie. Nitro comes and circles around our feet until he's passed out from all the excitement.

It's a chick flick, which usually makes me squirm, but I've seen this one before and actually found it somewhat entertaining. Annie and her buddy are completely engrossed, so Baya and I snuggle up without reservation. She smooths her hand over my chest, and I snatch it up and bury a kiss in her palm.

"Wouldn't it be nice if we could do this when we got back?" she whispers. Her eyes sparkle in the light as she gives a weary smile.

"We will do this when we get back." I tighten my grip around her waist, and Baya slides over, filling in the gap between us. "It just might be a while before it actually happens." Cole pops to mind. We both know he's the only thing standing between the two of us enjoying a movie in one another's arms back at the apartment.

"I hate the thought of it being a while." She twirls her fingers through my hair.

"Me, too." I tuck my hand down under her shirt just enough to feel her warm, smooth skin. I'd hate for Annie to look back and see me feeling up my girlfriend, so I try to keep it discreet.

"Hey," I whisper brushing my lips over her brow. "You know what I just realized?"

"How much better the cookies taste because I made them?" She runs her fingers over my ribs, and I can feel a dull ache of pleasure trail all the way down to my balls.

"I won't contest that." I burrow my face into her neck. "But, actually, I was thinking—" On second thought it's ridiculous to announce to someone you consider them your girlfriend. It's funny, though, because I've felt a strong connection to her right from the beginning.

"What?" She touches her finger over my lips, and the heat factor rises in my jeans. "Tell me, or I'll tickle you, and if you try to tickle me back, your sister and her friend will throw their shoes at your privates. It's girl code."

"They're not wearing any shoes." I nod over to their feet waving in the air as they lie on their bellies. "But, just in case they're within reach"—a small laugh rumbles from me as I touch my lips to her ear—"I was just thinking how special you are—how we're together. You know, you're my girlfriend." My Adam's apple rises and falls as I swallow hard. It takes all of my strength to keep thoughts of the past at bay. My finger floats to her mouth, and I trace out the smile taking over.

"Really?" She scoots her head onto my shoulder to get a better look at me. "I'm honored to be your girlfriend." She leans in and passes her lips over mine, soft as air. "Thank you."

"I'm the thankful one," I blow it hot in her ear.

Baya tucks in closer until she's partially sitting on my lap, and my dick does its best to salute her.

Shit. I move a little to the left to divert a full-blown situation from presenting itself, but Baya jumps on board without hesitating, and I pull her in close, hoping she won't notice.

"Someone is happy to see me." Her bottom lip curves into a delicious smile. "You want to take this party someplace else?"

"I would if I felt like I could walk across the room." I seal my lips over her neck.

The movie ends in a blur. But I couldn't focus on it anyway, not with Baya taking up all my available brain cells—the rush of blood she's sending to stray parts of my body. Not that I mind. I plan on reverting all of my focus to Baya from now on. It feels good to love someone again—and to have them love me back.

"You want to get to bed?" I pull her up off the couch.

"I thought you'd never ask."

6

Stay with Me Play with Me

Baya

It's quiet in the Edwards' home after midnight. Annie and her friend are clear down the hall, and I have no clue where his mother's room is in conjunction to Bryson's, but that's not going to stop me, or my quivering parts, from bunking up with him.

I brush my teeth and change into something a lot more comfortable—a hell of a lot easier to take off on command like my tank top and Whitney Briggs boy-shorts that barely hug my hips. But for the sake of trekking down the hall, I don a cardigan that acts as a robe.

I give a gentle knock over his door and it cracks open, exposing his gorgeous denim-blue eyes smiling back at me. If he thinks I'm letting a perfectly good Bryson Edwards go to waste tonight, he's got another thing coming—hopefully him—and, greedily, me.

"Who is it?" He gravels it out low and deep.

"Girl Scout. I come bearing cookies."

"Well, then." The door glides open. "Who the hell am I to turn down a Girl Scout?" Bryson pulls me in with a devilish gleam in his eye. He locks the door behind us and flicks off the lights. The moon filters into the room and washes the floor—his *bed* in a steady cascade of winter white, pale as a blanket of snow. "Come here," he whispers as his lips press over mine. He walks me backward over to the mattress until we fall onto it with him lying beside me. I swim up to his pillow and nestle my head into it. The entire room smells clean like fabric softener and bleach as if the sheets were just changed.

"Comfy," I muse.

"So where are the cookies?"

"Would you believe that I'm hiding them somewhere on my person, and it's up to you to find them?" I lift my knee over his back and rub down to his thigh, hard and steady.

"It's on." He growls it out sexy as hell. "I'm planning an extensive search, but I doubt I'll find them."

"That's because you already ate them—greedy bastard."

Bryson lights up the room with a dark laugh and pulls me in tight with his hand heavy on my bottom. "I am a greedy bastard. I want all of you."

I take him in like this, sheer perfection.

He's right here, and I want nothing more than to close the gap between us until he falls into me. I'm boiling over, ready to have him, ready for him to have me any way he wishes.

I stretch my arms up over my head and wriggle my body into his mattress.

His chest ticks with a silent laugh. "Whatever it is you're doing, keep doing it." A seam of moonlight catches his features, exposing the fact he clearly approves.

"I'm settling in." I twist my hips into the bed. "I think I could get a good night's sleep here."

"Oh sweetie"—he growls it out as the smile slides off his face —"if you spent the night in my room, there wouldn't be a whole hell of a lot of sleeping going on." His fiery breath sears over my mouth like a promise. "And, if you did happen to fall asleep, I'd be guilty of doing something very, very wrong."

My fingers run down his granite-like abs and unbutton his jeans. I glide down the bed and plant a kiss just above his boxers.

"I don't plan on sleeping," I say it low like a threat. "And neither should you."

His cheek flexes on one side and a dimple depresses.

Holy crap. Bryson is going to have me writhing on his bed before he ever touches me. That sweet spot between my legs spasms in agreement.

"God, you're gorgeous," I whisper, lifting my hand to conform to his features.

"Hey, that's my line." He picks my hand up and presses a wet kiss over my finger.

"Is it just a line?" I take him in like this, under the supervision of a powder soft moon.

"It's never just a line," he moans as his milk-white teeth skim over his lip. "Everything I say to you is the God's honest truth." His chin dips just a notch. "You,

Baya, are fit to be hewn from marble. Every artist, every poet should be so lucky to venerate your beauty. You're a work of art, straight from the master. Every woman on the planet should lament the fact she's not you." He swallows loud with a click, and his hand shakes as it settles over my cheek. "I want you, Baya." His voice trembles.

"I want you, too." I take in a breath and wait for something unexpected to happen.

His mouth opens slightly, and for a second, I think he's going to devour me—I *pray* that he will.

"I want to be with you," I say it plain as day in the event there was any confusion. "Now would be nice," I whisper. I don't think I could make it any clearer unless he prefers a physical cue, and dear God that is the very next step. I reach down and dip my hand into his jeans, touching the soft curls at the base of his boxers.

"Baya." His eyes close a moment as his features grow all too serious, his smile melts away like candle wax. Bryson pulls me out slowly, as if he were an unwilling partner in evicting my fingers. "You don't want it like this." He shakes his head just barely. "Not with my mom and sister down the hall. I want your first time to be incredible." He dots each of my fingers with a kiss, and a line of fire tracks down each one of them. "If you feel the need to scream out my name, and you will—" he holds his finger over my lips, his expression vexingly sober—"I want you to feel free—unrestrained."

A moan escapes me at the thought of shouting out his name, hell, just being near him like this feels like a privilege.

"I guess you're right." I swim back up to him. "And, for the record, waiting is just this side of torture." I nudge his foot with mine. "But that doesn't mean I can't spend the night, right?"

He traces his hand over mine, slow, like honey dripping off my skin. "I'll be the last person to kick you out of bed." Bryson tucks his chin and looks demonically sexy from this angle. It makes me want him twice as bad.

"I guess it's better that nothing serious happens. I'm not ready to disappoint you just yet."

His head ticks back a notch. "You could never disappoint me." He runs his finger down the curve of my cheek, melts it down past my neck and stops just shy of my cleavage.

"Yeah, well, I'm sure it'll be awkward, so I apologize in advance for dragging you to the Baya-loses-her-virginity party." I glance down at my shorts a moment. "I want to know everything. I want you to teach me."

"Hey." Bryson scoots in until his body adheres to mine and rides his warm hand up and down my back. "There's no party I'd rather be at." He cinches a sad smile in his cheek. "And believe me, if I weren't invited I'd be pretty ticked." He rumbles in my ear with a kiss. His heart beats over my shoulder like a hammer, straight to the bone. "And I *will* teach you. Trust me, I plan on leaving no stone unturned. It will be a thorough, thorough lesson. I promise." He holds up a hand like a Boy Scout. "You're going to be amazing. I already know this." Bryson growls into his words as if there were a psychotically sexy threat imbedded in there somewhere, and my insides cinch.

"Teach me, slowly." I pull his hand over my chest until he clasps on and offers a firm squeeze. "I'm ready for my first lesson."

"I suppose there's a lot we can do before..." His words drift in the air like musical notes, stretching across the wall like erotic shadows you could touch and feel. Bryson runs his fingers under my tank top and skims over my nipples, and my back arches at his touch.

"You're so incredibly beautiful, you know that?" His mouth covers mine with a sweet kiss that elevates me to that perfect nirvana just this side of ecstasy. My breathing grows erratic. My hips migrate to his just hoping he'll break all the carnal rules he's imposed tonight.

I stream a series of kisses up to his ear. "Do you have protection?" There's not one part of me that believes he's not into this.

"Not in the vicinity." He pumps a dry grin. "And it's a good thing, or I'd be unstoppable."

Perfect. This is going to put my body and mind in a sexual paralysis without any hope for release. Bryson rolls on top of me and pulls up on his elbows until his lips hover just above mine. His breath holds the scent of minty toothpaste. He's clean and mean, and I'm pretty sure I can't take much more of this sexual depravation.

Hopefully he won't mind too much when I start dry humping him for the hell of it.

"I like you hot and bothered." He grins from his aerial perspective. His eyes illuminate in the dim light and glow like that of a tiger. "When the time comes"—he bears into me in earnest—"I'm going to run my mouth over every single inch of you." His finger traces the outline of my shoulder, down through my ribs, then my hips. He moves lower still all the way down between my thighs, and a small cry escapes my throat. My girl parts are ticking like a bomb, begging and *shouting* the only way they know how for me to get him the hell down there a.s.a.p. He rubs his fingers over my panties, hard, and I buck into him. "I'm going to sink a kiss right here."

I hadn't thought about Bryson kissing me anywhere but my lips, and now an entire world of possibility had opened, new fears were springing to life, and, not surprisingly, my vagina is weeping with joy. Maybe it's a good thing we didn't dive into anything tonight. It's becoming clear that a scalding shower and the business end of a razor are going to be mandatory for this new adventure with Bryson.

"Come here." He turns me in his arms until my hips conform to his stomach, and we're happily spooning. "Love you, Baya. Sleep tight."

"I love you, too, Bryson."

But I don't get any sleep. I just revel in the fact that I'm in Bryson Edwards' arms—in his bed, and I want to memorize how it feels.

Soon the weekend will be over, and all I'll have is a memory.

❧❦

In the morning, well, technically the afternoon, when we finally stop resisting the idea of spending all day in bed holding one another, we shower and dress.

Annie and her friend are already out of the house, and so is his mother.

Bryson and I decide to take in a movie in the late afternoon, then in the evening check out the fall festival that's taken over the pumpkin fields down the street from his house. There's a Ferris wheel and rides that are guaranteed to make you regurgitate your dinner—entire rows of carnival games that are rigged to suck the change straight from your pocket.

We watch as a boy effortlessly knocks down a pyramid of milk cans and wins a four-foot tall, hot pink giraffe. He kisses its nose before handing it off to the shy girl by his side.

"*Aww*," I coo, gripping Bryson's shoulder. "That was so sweet! Those things are impossible to do."

"Impossible?" His head ticks back a notch. "Just let me know right now if you want a hot pink giraffe because, if you do, it's as good as yours." He gives my waist a quick squeeze.

"Oh"—a quiet laugh bubbles in my chest—"you think you're that good, do you?"

"Oh, sweetie"—Bryson's chest thumps as he comes in close with a dark smile—"I know I am." He's bedroom eyeing me, and I'm almost positive we're not talking about pink giraffes anymore.

"I double dog dare you to prove it." Both in and out of the bedroom.

Bryson digs out a couple of bills and starts in on a pitching adventure that seems to span hours even if it is only a few minutes. I laugh my ass off as he struggles to knock the bottles down, only managing to knock one or two from the top at a time.

"I think you should aim for the bottom," I say.

"I am." He looks bewildered that his technique is failing and so miserably at that.

"Here let me try." I take one of the weighted beanbags from him, and the top bottle doesn't even budge once I hit it. "Hey, this thing is rigged. I nailed that sucker. Those things must weigh forty pounds each. It's never going to work. It's impossible."

Bryson pinches his lips together. He washes those sky-born eyes over mine and gives a tiny grin.

"You make everything possible, Baya." He hands over another dollar and steps back with his ammo locked and loaded like he's about to throw the most important pitch at the world series. "This one's for you, girl." He heaves the beanbag at the poor defenseless bottles, and all three of them explode backward like a nuclear detonation.

"You did it!" I squeal.

"*You* did it." Bryson wraps his arms around me and lands a warm kiss over my cheek. My stomach flutters. It cycles up and down as if we were on the most harrowing roller coaster, and it feels like bliss.

The man behind the counter hands me an oversized giraffe that glows the most obnoxious color known to man—bright neon pink.

"I think I'll put this in my old dorm, right on my bed. You think Jeanie will notice?"

"What? You can't part with her. We're practically parents now." He gives my ribs a slight tickle as we head back down the midway. "We'll have to take her wherever we go and get a sitter while we're in class."

A soft laugh streams from me as I slip an arm around his waist.

"We should name her." I lay my head on his shoulder, and, oddly, I can feel his body go rigid beneath me. I glance up, and his eyes are fixed straight ahead, his face bleached out pale as a paper white moon. "I said we should name her." I jostle him by the waist in an effort to pull him out of his trance. "Hey, are you okay?"

A tall, lanky guy makes his way over with a girl in spiked heels that dig into the dirt each time she takes a step.

"Well if it isn't Bryson fucking Edwards." His dark eyes look serious—no smile. He offers Bryson a knuckle bump, and he's slow to reciprocate. "How's it going?" His gaze drifts over to me. I can feel his eyes wandering over my features, sizing me up before glancing at the overgrown animal tucked under my arm. There's something familiar about him, but I can't quite pinpoint it.

"It's going." Bryson loosens his grip over me until his arm falls to his waist.

The boy holds out a hand in my direction. "I'm Grant."

"Baya." I offer a firm shake. He holds my gaze, heavy as anchors, until finally the hint of a tragic smile breaks through.

"It's really nice to meet you, Baya." His eyes sweep the ground a moment.

The girl at his side picks at the cotton candy in her hand, and, for the most part, ignores the entire exchange.

Grant cuts a look to Bryson that says something just beneath the surface. "It's nice you're doing good—moving on with your life. Not everyone gets that chance." He shakes his head as they make their way into the crowd.

Bryson blows a breath through his cheeks as if he had been holding it the entire time.

It hits me why he looks so familiar. "That was about that girl in the picture, wasn't it?" He had the same dark hair, same serious eyes.

"That was her brother."

Bryson and I head to the truck.

He doesn't say anything all the way home.

ℰℒℬℭℬ

By the time we get back to the house, there's a seam of tangerine sky melting over the horizon. I decide not to push anything on the subject of what I'm presuming is his ex-girlfriend. Something tells me she was never a notch on his wall. But a part of me wonders if he'll ever be ready to talk about her—if deep down I really want him to.

His phone buzzes as soon as we hit the house, and he examines it with a widening grin on his face.

"You win the lottery?" I tease, landing the giraffe on a stool in the entry.

"Something like that." His eyes lower to mine. A fire burns in them, and it's all for me. Bryson holds up his phone victoriously. "My dad had an emergency at the Ice Bar, and my mom is graciously spending the night up there to help out with the details. Refrigeration unit is down. The place is literally melting." His chest rumbles at the thought.

"Do you have to go?"

"And miss out on us having the house all to ourselves? Not a chance."

My heart thumps so loud I can practically hear it reverberating off the walls. "What about Annie?" There's a slight rise of panic brewing in me. Tonight might be the night, and, now, all I can think about is how I'm going to sneak off and shave my legs—not to mention more intricate and delicate places that he talked about landing those lips on. Those kisses he talked about last night made my skin flush and my toes curl in every good way. I can't imagine doing that with Bryson. It scares and exhilarates me all at the same time.

Bryson leans in. His hotter-than-hell smile takes over for just a moment.

"Annie is spending the night at Kaya's house." He brushes his finger over the side of my cheek, and an electrical current races through me.

Holy *shit*.

"What do you think we should do?" My voice shakes as I ask the question. My mind races with all kinds of deliciously pornographic possibilities. My head feels light and fuzzy, and suddenly it feels as if I could pass out if I wanted.

Okay. Don't panic. If he green-lights operation deflower-power I'll simply jump in the shower. Then I'll put on my Whitney Briggs shorts—no wait, I wore those last night. I think I have a pair of thongs, but then I might as well be naked, and, for sure, I don't have a decent bra for him to see me in. Crap. This is never going to work. Wait, people don't wear clothes while having sex, so all of the aforementioned fashion blunders aren't even necessary. My body pulsates like one giant heartbeat while my girl parts pound against my brain trying to get me on board with the idea of sleeping with him tonight.

"What do you think we should do?" He tucks his head back a notch, and I can tell he's holding back the urge to smile.

"I think I should shower." Did I just say that out fucking loud? He's going to think I'm gross—that I *smell*. "I mean shave." Shit! Shit! Shit! He's going to think I have an entire Canadian forest tucked between my legs, God only knows he'd be right. "I mean, I guess—we should change into our PJs and maybe we could eat cookies." PJs? *Cookies?* Perfect. Let him know you have the dress code and diet of a three-year-old—that ought to turn him on. NOT. Way to show him you're not Cole's kid sister.

"Hmm." His cheek cinches up one side while I boil in a vat of self-inflicted embarrassment. And, worst of all, I can tell he's enjoying this. "That's quite a hygienic, albeit nutritiously deficient, agenda you have mapped out." Bryson wraps his arms around my waist and sways me as if we were dancing. "Why don't you put on your bathing suit?" He sears a kiss over the rim of my ear. "I'll whip us up something to eat, and we can hit the hot tub. Does that sound good?"

"Sounds more than good." At least he's able to think intelligently under the circumstances, unlike me who's reduced herself to a walking ball of hormones on fire. Then again, he's done this a million times. Of course he's going to be way more casual about the whole thing. Food then sex. He's had a steady diet of both for the last few years. I'm just too much of a dumbass to realize the fact that's how most people round out their day.

God, that's going to be my new routine with Bryson! *Gah!* I just want to scream and shake people. Well, not Bryson, *other* people who don't seem to realize how fucking fantastic the rest of my life is going to be. I should call Mom! No wait, ixnay on the calling of the mother. Although, one day, in a land far far away, she'll be ecstatic for me.

I scoot upstairs with my thighs quivering every step of the way and jump into the shower, attacking every part of me below the neck that has hair with a razor as I try my best to banish and sculpt. After several nicks and close run-ins with a few surface veins, I dig through my bag and pull out my red two-piece that I had no idea I would even be needing, but, since I have my entire existence in this bag, here it is. I toss a long sweater over it and head back down, barefoot.

"In here." He calls from the dining room, and my private parts quiver as if telling me to hurry the hell up and get that boy on top of me already. Bryson has a series of candles set out and two plates brimming with what looks like ramen noodles.

"Aren't you the master chef?" I tease while taking a seat next to him.

"I am." He pours sparkling water into a pair of tall goblets and slides one over to me. "I guess I'm more of a minute chef tonight. I blame that on a serious lack of food in the fridge."

I try to take a few bites, but my stomach has already gone into lockdown. There's no way I'll be able to eat another bite. I glance up at Bryson, and he hasn't taken those steel-colored eyes off me once.

"You ready to hit the hot tub?" He gives a devious smile as if he had arranged for the mishap at the Ice Bar himself.

"I thought you'd never ask."

Bryson leads us out to a gloriously-huge backyard that spans in every direction with emerald-rolling lawns. A cabana sits tucked close to the house with an expansive patio around it, and nestled in the middle is an oversized hot tub.

In the distance, a trail of bright green lights blink on and off under a juniper tree and it takes a moment to register what they are.

"Look!" I marvel.

"Fireflies." He lands a kiss in the hollow of my neck, and I take a breath.

"It looks like magic," I say, panting into him. Bryson, plus fireflies, plus hot tub equals a trifecta of perfection. My vagina pounds against my thighs because I forgot to add penis in the trifecta mathematics. It's a rather focused event taking place down there, and now I'm blushing for no reason.

Bryson turns on the lights to the hot tub, and the water glows a glacial blue just like his eyes.

"You're magic, Baya." He helps me into the bubbling water, and it sears over my skin like a heated glove as I sink into it.

Bryson lands beside me as we look out at the deep navy night. My heart feels like it's about to riot right out of my chest, and my thighs tremble for his touch. I can't believe that the rest of the world feels this way—this fucking *fantastic* right before they experience one of the most intimate moments of their lives. And something in me wants to believe that being with Bryson would be exactly this incredible night after night. I know for a fact it would be.

"What are you thinking?" He slips his hand around my waist and pulls me into his lap. My thigh grazes over the bump in his trunks, and everything enlivens in me from the waist down. The Notorious V.A.G. that sits tucked between my legs screams like a cheerleader at the Super Bowl just waiting for that final touch down. The girls sort of want to get in on the action, too, so I position them over his chest and gently rub his marble hewn body with mine.

"I might die if you don't kiss me soon." True story. I leave out the part that I might go into a bona fide cardiac arrest if my heart beats any faster from anticipation—that my uterus is threatening to explode like a pressure cooker, and my nipples are trying to claw their way out of my swimsuit. My hormones are about to take a violent turn for the worse if he doesn't work his magic over me soon. My legs are already willing to part for him. I'm so hungry, so curious to see what it might feel like to have him in me, a part of me wants to cry.

"Well, then, I'd better kiss you." His eyes grow all too serious, and he comes in for the kill. "Baya." He shakes his head. "Don't feel like we have to do anything tonight. I'm not like that. We can take our time. I promise,

I'm not going anywhere." He touches his nose to mine before landing a spark of a kiss on my lips, and every ounce of me feels like its about to boil over in a lust-fueled meltdown.

"I want to." I glance down at the water a second. "I wish I knew what I was doing. I'd give anything to have your track record right now." I give a nervous laugh while scratching at his chest. "Okay, well maybe not so extensive but a little experience wouldn't hurt." Like a dozen or so tally marks worth.

"Are you kidding? I've got nothing but respect for you for waiting. You should. You're worth the wait, Baya. And the fact you want to share something as special as your first time with me makes me feel honored. I hope you'll share *every* time with me." He pulls my chin up gently with his finger and steadies his eyes over mine. "I want to be your first and your last," he whispers. "I'm glad you waited. And, trust me, I wish I would have waited for you, too."

My heart melts, and I memorize him like this, vulnerable, perfect in every way.

"So why the long line of girls?" I've been wondering for weeks, outside of mass amounts of testosterone, why so many different girls when just a few repeats could have sufficed? "I've counted those notches, by the way." I lean in and take a gentle bite over his lip. He feels full and slippery between my teeth, and I resist the urge to pierce right through. "You're nearing triple digits."

"Triple, huh?" He gives a long blink. "The only thing that could ever explain that long line of girls is the fact I'm an asshole." His chest rumbles beneath me. A cute little dimple digs in just shy of his lips, and a wildfire rips through me, running its flames between my legs, licking me with its scorching hot tongue. "I was trying to numb the pain." His eyes cloud over with grief. "But with you, there's no more pain to numb. You wiped it away that first day I met you, and I couldn't explain it. I knew right then I needed you in my life."

"I've always suspected my boobs held superpowers." I sink a little in the water because obviously now is no time for jokes, but I'm lame that way. I can't help it. Now it's me who feels like the asshole. "Sorry."

"No." He gives a weak laugh. Bryson pulls my legs over his hips and spins me in the water. "I swear that's why I love you. You have the ability to pull me out of the pit, and you don't even know it." He presses another kiss to my lips, and I can feel him swallow hard. "Just when I'm about to go under, you pull me out. Not any one of those girls I've been with before had the ability to do that. They were just taking up space while I tried to hide my feelings."

His eyes dance over mine as a moment of silence ticks by.

"If it didn't help, then why bed your way through the Greek alphabet? You're a nice guy, Bryson. It doesn't really seem like you." I wrap my finger around a curl at the base of his neck and give a gentle tug.

"I don't know." His gaze drifts past me. "I thought for so long I didn't deserve anyone. I figured if I satisfied my itch that would be all I'd ever need—all I could ever really have. I didn't want to ruin anybody's life." His eyes fill with tears, and he blinks them away. We've crossed that invisible line, and I'm about to lose him again, so I reel him back in.

"Bryson—you deserve everything that life has to offer, especially love—especially the love of a very special someone. I hope I can be that someone for you."

"You already are." His arms collapse around my back as he holds me tight. "And I wouldn't want to share my life with anyone else—just you, Baya. I mean it."

Bryson pulls me in by the face and lands a kiss over my lips, slow and sweet at first until it builds to something fantastically stronger, far more hungrier than any of the kisses we've ever shared before. His hands ride down until he's riding hard circles over my nipples through my bathing suit. A soft moan escapes me, vibrating from my lips to his. His hot mouth melts over my neck and down to the cleft of my shoulder. I can feel his cool breath, his hot kisses, and a powerful pang of pleasure shoots through my body, starting from the most intimate part of me.

"Do you want this with me, Baya?" Bryson pulls back and examines me as if he wasn't quite sure he could simply trust the words streaming from my lips. He needs to see the evidence on my face because he knows I can't hide my feelings for him, and I can't.

"Yes," I whisper directly into his mouth as a smile forms on my lips. "God, yes."

Bryson melts over me with a kiss—his erratic breathing, his racing heart all let me know he wants this too. His hand rides down low and glides slowly into the front of my bathing suit bottom.

I let out an audible moan, and my neck bends back from his touch.

Bryson pulls me up as a naughty grin rides low on his lips. "How about we move this show upstairs?"

I bite down on a smile. "I double dog dare you."

My lose-your-virginity party is about to begin, and the guest of honor just put all of my pleasure zones on erotic notice.

I have a feeling this is going to be the best damn party of my life.

ಐOಚ

Bryson scoops me up, once I have the towel secured over me. It's freezing out, but my body is happily numb with shock at the prospect of what he might do to it. He whisks us through the house and up the stairs, wasting no time in getting us to his bedroom.

He kicks the door shut behind us, and it sounds off like a clap of thunder. The moonlight illuminates the room even brighter than it did last night.

"Baya." He pulls his lips over mine, rough and needy—and, dear God, do I ever want to give him what he needs. The incessant urge to giggle crops up, and I shoo it away like a field mouse in the kitchen.

"Last chance if you want off this train," he offers. "We could go downstairs and watch TV—play Scrabble if you want."

Scrabble? I wonder how many points I could score for f-u-c-k-i-n-g? Not that it would be the type of "score" I'm hoping for.

I belt out a laugh. "Maybe we could round out the night working on crossword puzzles together?" God, he'd better not say yes.

His chest vibrates over mine as he pulls me to the bed. We sit on our knees and face each other, our chests still heaving from the excitement, the *exertion,* to get here. Bryson takes me in from his vantage point in an observational way as if I were a new scientific discovery.

"I'll work on crossword puzzles with you until we're old and grey if you let me." His cheek rides high on one side.

"I like the old and grey part." I pick up his hand and intertwine our fingers. "But, right now, I think we should stick to the original plan of action, and I do mean action." I pull his hand to my mouth and graze over his fingers.

"Sounds like you're pretty focused." His teeth illuminate in the dark like mirrors.

"I'm focused one hundred percent on you, Bryson Edwards." I brush away any apprehension I might have and hold him by the back of the neck. "Will you love me tonight?"

He swallows hard never losing our stare. "I'll love you every night for the rest of your life if you let me, Baya Brighton." Bryson lands his lips over mine with a series of boiling kisses that promise a thousand tomorrows all their own. Bryson gently removes the towel from around me and peels off his shorts without his lips ever losing touch with mine.

My insides squeeze until it feels as if I'm going to be sick. I pull back and look at him like this, naked as he bears himself to me. The quiet light of the moon settles over his skin, and I can see the ripples in his cut abs, his chest, the cut V just below his abs, then below that, every last inch— Oh. My. God.

Oh my God, oh my God, oh my *God!*

Bryson Edwards has a beam between his legs. An *Olympic* sized balance beam, and I half-expect to see an entire string of gymnasts burst into the room with team USA leotards on and break out into a routine over it.

Just fuck. There is no way in hell he's ever going to fit inside me. He's going to impale me if he tries. One good thrust, and he'll shoot right out my throat. I can just see the paramedic ride to hospital now. Crap. I'm going to end up on YouTube and Instagram, Vine, and all sorts of social network sites as the girl who cracked in half while trying to lose her virginity. I'll be the poster child for abstinence at Catholic schools the world over. I'll be on Reddit, then the news, and my mother will see me and kill

ADDISON MOORE

me, no wait, Cole will beat her to it right after he snaps off
that branch hanging from Bryson's body.

I take a breath in sheer terror at the thought of what
might come next. I must be deformed. Other girls must
have a ditch you could back a dump truck in. And poor
me, I have a hell of a time just inserting a slender tampon.
This is never going to work. If I knew there was anything
wrong with me, I would never have gotten his hopes, or
his tree limb up, in the first place.

Bryson takes my hand and runs my fingers over the
length of it. He's hot to the touch, hard as steel, more rigid
than I imagined, and a little skin cap sits at the top like a
crown.

I'd say something that plays into our big bad wolf
meme like *my what a long penis you have.* But I'm
deathly afraid he'd come back with something like, *the
better to spear you with.*

My fingers tighten around him, and Bryson bends
his head back and sucks in a quick breath. I can make out
the ridge of his Adam's apple rising and falling like a
shadow.

"Did I hurt you?" I let go as if snatching it back from
a rattle snake.

"No." His lips curl as he says it, and he returns my
hand to the foot-long splitting the difference between us.
"I could come right now if I'm not careful." He presses the
words out with an ache as if he were in pain on some level.
Bryson reaches over and unties my bathing suit top, extra
slow, as if he were reveling in the moment. My body

flinches as he whips it away. Here I am, on my knees, in front of Bryson Edwards the king of mattress tag at Whitney Briggs, and I'm ready to take that next step with him. Well, most of me is ready. My squeezebox is seriously reconsidering the idea.

Bryson reaches down and unties my bikini bottom and pulls it off slow through the front, and the fabric rubs along the most intimate part of me like a slick, wet tongue.

A moan works its way up my throat, and I try to cap it. I don't want him to think this is all too much for me, that I'm overwhelmed in any way—of course, I am, but in every *good* way. The truth is the simple act of him stripping me nude is far more erotic than I could have ever imagined, and that vulnerable part of me is back on board with the idea.

"I'm going to make love to you, Baya."

A tiny squeal escapes from me, more fear than cheer, but I doubt he heard over the bongo drum-like riot, taking place in my chest.

His fingers feather over my cheek, and I move toward him like a magnet. Bryson's heated hands roam over my back. He rounds out the front and gives my nipples a gentle pinch before dipping a hand down to my thighs and finding his way into the warmth of my body. I seal a breath off in my lungs and let out a hearty, yet vocally impaired, groan as my sweet spot jumps up and down in his hand as if it were happy to finally meet him.

"Oh, yeah," he groans. "You're so wet."

"That's because we were in the hot tub," I whisper through a smile.

A dull laugh pumps from him. "And here I thought you were ready for me."

Ready for him. Right. Crap. I'm such a moron. Who the hell did I think I was sleeping with Bryson without at least brushing up on my sexual terminology? I'm beyond ridiculous to think I was just going to causally pick things up as we went along. I should have logged hours watching porn instead of reading Yates for Lit. It's like I've got no fucking priorities. I should have read the *Karma Sutra*—shoved it in Cole's face when he asked what I was reading. How do you like my book boyfriend now, bitch?

I shake my head, quickly chasing away the desire to inadvertently tell off my brother—from *thinking* of my brother while my newfound boyfriend's hand is rubbing me the right way.

Bryson bows his head into me, his eyes close, his chest thumps with each breath. His fingers glide over my folds and I bury my lips in his neck as a dull cry rattles through me.

I let out a breath. Oh, *hell,* yes.

Bryson rubs over me slowly, methodically as if he had an entire game plan mapped out, and I am so loving the game plan. His fingers brush back until he carefully inserts one into me, and my hips writhe with pleasure right there in his hand. I crash my body against his and push my cheek into his shoulder with my mouth open and panting. My entire body demands to detonate over him.

This is something far stronger than those pansy-like quivers I've been experiencing, and just the thought that he can elicit in me an excitement I had no idea existed makes my muscles twitch with ecstasy.

"You're so tight," he whispers close in my ear, gliding his finger in and out.

I try to agree with him, but I'm biting down over my lips, outright refusing to open my mouth in fear a viral scream will leap from my lungs. He's loving me, touching me in ways that I could never imagine, and I'd hate to break the magic with the unearthly shriek begging to rip from my vocal cords.

Bryson peppers my face with a soft string of kisses. His hand moves inside me spiraling deeper until it feels as if he's going to touch my belly. "Does that feel good, baby?"

A small choking sound evicts itself from my throat.

"Mmm," he moans softly in my ear with a kiss. "I thought so. I love watching you. You're fucking beautiful when you're about to come, you know that?"

Oh God. As if being in bed with Bryson wasn't enough, he has to go and turn up the dirty talk. And I freaking LOVE the dirty talk!

My body bucks into his, and I hold onto his shoulders, digging my fingers into his flesh, trembling as a wash of heat takes over my body. I'm going to lose it right on his hand before we ever get to the part where he injects his tree trunk into me. I squeeze my eyes shut and throw my head back as he presses into my body with an earnest desire.

"Baya," he whispers as his voice drills through my spine—between my legs where his hand is still loving me, slow and purposeful.

Bryson lays me on the bed with his body hovering gently over mine. My head arches back as I push my hips to meet his. I'm writhing, unable to settle down. Each nerve in my body is raw and alive at his touch. My senses are at attention, every inch of my flesh is calling him to cover me like a sheet. A moan gets locked in my throat as he pulls his hand away, and a severe ache is left in his absence. Maybe this is as far as we'll ever get. Maybe he's already done the vaginal math, and he knows he'll never fit inside, so why bother trying.

Bryson touches his lips to my ear. He covers my lobe with his mouth and runs his tongue along the rim like an erotic warning.

"Bryson," I hiss, writhing from his volcanic-like kisses.

Just as I'm about to suggest he get the hell back down there, his hand covers me again. His finger glides in and out, and a sweet throb rockets through me, slow and steady as he picks up his pace.

He presses a kiss to my ear. "I want you to come for me, Baya," it streams like an inferno from his mouth.

A breath gets caught in my throat as he plunges deep inside me, his thumb moves over my folds, and I let out a breath as I flex into him. I'm shaking so hard, the entire bed rattles.

"But not like this," he whispers. A quiet laugh filters through his chest. Bryson reaches up and cups my breasts again, his hand still wet from touching me. He presses me together and buries his lips between the soft mounds of flesh for a moment. He sears his mouth across my chest until his lips are secured over one, and gives a playful bite before sucking on it careful and slow. He lands his teeth gently over my nipple and pulls it out, stretching it until it feels as if I'm about to burst. "Did you like that?" He teases as he rides his lips up toward mine.

"Yes." I can barely manage the word as I lose myself in his kisses.

"Good." He slips his fingers below my waist. "Now I'm going to make you come, Baya." He lies me back and rises above me. "In my mouth."

Did he just say his *mouth*?

I take in a breath and can't seem to shut off the intake valve.

His mouth is like twelve times better than his hand, not that there was anything wrong with Bryson's hand. God no. It should be cast in a mold and sold at those naughty adult stores worldwide. It would be a best seller because each finger holds its own magical property. I have a feeling that little joy toy would turn the entire vibrator market on its ear—penis, whichever.

"Do you want that?" He smolders over me with his bedroom eyes, a ghost of a smile playing on his lips. A sharp sting ignites over me when he asks the question.

I let out a little whimper because, holy shit, YES I motherfucking want that. I give a little nod in the event my whimper could be misconstrued in any way, shape, or form.

A wild prickle of excitement tracks over my skin as every cell in my body cheers him on.

Bryson trails his kisses down to my chest, and I jump with each one. These weren't just any kisses, these were blazing a trail to a place where no mouth has ever ventured before. He lands his lips over my nipple one more time, and it melts from his heated tongue before he dives lower still, burying a kiss in my belly. My eyes flutter back in my head, and all sorts of feel good vibrations rocket through me like errant missiles shooting off in every direction at once.

Oh God, the belly kiss. Yes—God yes, the *belly* kiss.

"*Bryson,*" I groan and hold him there for a second.

"Does that feel good?" He sinks lower, not waiting for an answer and pushes my knees apart until I feel vulnerable, and my entire lower half spasms from sheer titillation.

My heart gyrates its way into my throat. I glance down and notice he's paused his efforts.

God, something's wrong. I knew it, I'm deformed down there, and now he wants nothing to do with me and my misshapen vagina. Or maybe he can't find it because I didn't take the time to do some serious landscaping. It was like hacking through swampland, and my poor razor dulled out before I could put a decent dent in the curly curtains. Crap. He's face to face with Furby and now he wants nothing more than to box it up and take me back to Boys "R" Us for a refund.

I hike up on my elbows and try to pull him back.

"Whoa." He snatches my hand and presses a hot kiss over one finger. "I'm just enjoying the view, honey. I'm not coming up for a while." He tucks a kiss into my inner thigh, and my vagina all but starts singing, *Welcome to the Jungle*. A sizzle of electricity spirals through me as his tongue tracks in a long hot line, closer and closer, to that tender part of me that's been waving him in like an air traffic controller since the day we met.

Oh God, he's going to do it. I fall back on the pillow and bite over my bottom lip until I'm sure I'm about to draw blood. I fist the covers, and my head twists back and forth in anticipation of where his searing lips might land next.

He pulls back up, and my sweet spot sags with disappointment.

"You're so fucking beautiful." He sinks a kiss just below my belly then trails his kisses further south, touching down over the dark triangle of hair, then below that, and I give a heated breath, then lower still until his lips press into the most tender part of me, and every ounce of estrogen in me screams *YES* because his rock star of a mouth just took center stage.

My head arches back, deliriously writhing into the pillow.

His tongue does a quick exploratory lay of the land, and I can feel him breathing over me. It sort of tickles in a deliciously sweet way. His teeth graze over me as he tracks lower, penetrating deep into me with his tongue, and I let out a fierce groan because, holy hell, I *so* was not expecting that.

WOW.

I twist my head until I bite down into my pillow. Bryson Edwards is killing me in the most erotic way possible. It's becoming painfully clear that I'm never going to survive this night. My heart is going to launch out of my throat at any moment because obviously I'm not designed to handle excitement of this caliber. Crap. I'm not even designed to handle a pedicure, what in the hell was I thinking climbing into bed with Bryson Edwards?

I have no idea how those countless girls he bedded ever survived the explosiveness of his lips, his body—the olive branch between his legs he's so ready and willing to extend. I bet there's some survivors group I can join after, that is if I manage to live through the endeavor, and we can all talk about how amazing the sex god of Whitney Briggs is in bed.

He runs his tongue along the slick between my thighs, and I groan as I grind my shoulders into the mattress. He lashes out over me until I'm clawing at the covers, scratching over his back, raking my fingers through his hair. His hand tracks down over my hips, and his finger finds its way inside me once again, this time with much more purpose and force behind it. His mouth remains steady over me while his hand pulsates in and out. I let out a fierce groan because it's all way too much more than this girl, or any of her parts, can handle.

The room starts in on a silent spin. My head and chest build with incredible pressure. That small space between my thighs has become the entire focus of my universe as an invisible blaze consumes me from the inside out.

Oh shit, shit—*shit*.

"*Bryson*." I lurch forward and spike my nails into his back. He plunges into me again with his hand and speeds up his tongue lashing efforts until I let out a scream that sears from my lungs, raw and urgent. "*Bryson!*" I lock my knees over his head half-afraid I'm going to crack his skull like a walnut, causing his brain to squirt into my lap. My body seizes and trembles until a dull ache rides through me, soothing and calm as the sea after a storm.

Bryson unleashes himself from the headlock and swims up beside me, his body slick with perspiration from the effort.

"You taste like sugar," he pants through a smile, still out of breath.

"Somehow I doubt that. But I appreciate the thought." I wrap my arms around him and press his sticky chest to mine.

"No really, you do. You're so fucking sweet." He tries to land his lips over mine, but I turn my head, deflecting his efforts to prove his carbohydrate-based theory. "I want you to taste it," he whispers while gently turning my head toward him. He lands a kiss over me before swiping his tongue in my mouth.

It tastes metallic, honeyed like an exotic nectar. I let Bryson love me with his tongue in my mouth while his breathing picks up pace as if he were about to step out onto the frontlines of battle and this were our final goodbye. Bryson singes his honeyed skin over mine, and I moan, running my hands over his drenched back.

He leans up on his elbow and examines me with a look of contentment for a small eternity.

"You said my name." He pins his cheek high on one side as he gently pushes the hair away from my face.

"I'm sure you're used to hearing your name cried out in ecstasy," I tease, pulling him in close by the small of his back.

"No one's ever said my name before, and I'm glad. I only want to hear it from you, ever." He sears another kiss off my lips, wet and juicy. Bryson reaches over to the nightstand and holds up a small foil packet. "You ready for round two?"

My stomach explodes in a ball of fire. "You think it's okay? I hate to sound naïve, but the lower forty-eight clearly have a bottleneck issue."

"Oh?" He pulls his lips to the side with a sarcastic flair. "Does that make these, Hawaii and Alaska?" He pinches each of my nipples in turn.

"Very funny."

"What were we discussing again?" He growls it out with a touch of a demonic laugh.

"The Panama Canal." I bite down over my lip before I start giggling like an idiot with no end in sight. It's happened before, the giggling thing. It derails me from the task at hand, and in no way do I want to be derailed while in bed with Bryson.

"Switching countries are we?" His eyes hood low as if he totally approves of the spontaneous geography lesson. "And, damn." He trails quick kisses to my belly and runs his hot tongue in a circle over it before dipping lower to the tangle of curls at the base of my body. "The Bermuda Triangle is just one of the many delicious destinations I plan on revisiting." He looks up as the smile melts from his face. "For the record, I'm suddenly very fucking interested in cartography."

I strangle out a laugh and pull him back up. "I don't know about round two. I'd hate to land in a wheelchair just because I'm physically inept."

"What?" He cinches back, looking more than slightly puzzled. "I promise, in no way are you inept. You're perfect in every way, shape, and form. Trust me, I'm in love with much more than your landscape. I'm in love with *you*, Baya—inside and out." He opens the foil package with his teeth and holds it to me. "You want to do the honors?"

"Um...okay." I take it from him and remove the sticky disc from inside. *Gah.* It's coated with syrup, and my fingers beg to get the hell away from it stat, but the

Pandora's Box of abnormally small secrets that's buried between my legs, begs for me to carry on with the endeavor. "This is sort of disgusting." A laugh bubbles from me, but I mean every word.

"Like this." Bryson guides me down over him and helps roll it out the length of his surprisingly oversized fifth appendage. I let my fingers run over the ridges before covering him with the sticky film.

"This is weird." I bite my lip, trying to ignore the fact my hands are covered with goo.

"Hold on girl." Bryson carefully draws me in by the cheeks. "Because it's about to get a whole lot better." He offers a tender kiss, and a burst of adrenaline spikes through me. Bryson gently presses my knees back until I open for him, wide and exposed. "That's my girl." He lies over me, and I take his weight as his breathing picks up another notch. "Don't let me hurt you," he pants, propping himself on his elbows.

I'd hate to break it to him, but that seems a non-contestable point right about now. There is no way in hell he's not going to hurt me. In fact, at this stage of the game, the question is just how much damage is he going to inflict? And should I have a team of plastic surgeons on standby ready to reconstruct my body.

"I want you to guide me in." He licks a heated line up my cheek.

I brace myself as I reach down to provide my less-than-enthusiastic navigational services.

Good God, he's the size of a freaking cucumber—one of those abnormally long and thick ones that makes you look twice in the supermarket because, deep down, you know it's vulgar. A whimper escapes my throat. I've seen enough television—enough R rated movies to know that some women scream their heads off during sex, and now it makes total sense why. It was the pain making them turn up the volume on their vocal cords—not pleasure. Although, this *is* Bryson inflicting the pain. On second thought, it will very much be pleasure. If there's a fine line between pleasure and pain, God knows I'm about to cross it in the very best way.

Bryson reaches down to help speed along the efforts. Obviously, he's got a hard-on to contend with, and I'm the one who foolishly volunteered to help relieve it.

"Right there," he whispers as the tip pushes its way into me.

My mouth opens, and a choking sound emits as he pushes in ever so slowly, and my existence feels like it's about to split open, ass first. My body takes him, hugs him, *strangles* him to be exact as he slowly fills me with his inexplicably long cucumber-like body.

Then, in a moment, he glides in deeper, and my insides wrap around him like a glove. A burning sensation rips through me in every direction at once, and a white-hot pain ignites where my ass once happily sat—and, horror of all horrors, tears come to my eyes. I press my lips tight, not wanting to ruin the moment as I resist the urge to slap him the hell away from me. Then he pulls out and offers a touch of relief before spearing back in, nice and slow, and, to my surprise, it begins to feels pleasurable through the pain.

"Tell me if I'm hurting you," he pants through a smile as he watches from above.

"No." As in, *no I won't*. Instead, I clutch onto his back and press him deeper until he hits the limit, and I let out a little cry of relief because he didn't pierce through my diaphragm and take out my vocal cords in the process. The smile melts off his face. His eyes roll into his head. His neck bends back a moment, and I give a private smile at the thought of reducing him to such a primal state of being.

"Oh shit, Baya," he groans, loud and proud of the way I'm making him feel, and now I'm glad his mother isn't anywhere near the house to listen in on our carnal vocal exchange.

"Bryson." I tighten my muscles around his joystick, and he pants a dull laugh.

"Yeah, that," he moans, before lowering his lips to mine. I reach back and press him in deeper still, folding my legs over his back and caging him in like seasoned pro.

Bryson takes in a quick breath and bites down over his lip.

There. I did it.

We did it.

I'm no longer Baya Brighton the perennial virgin, I'm Bryson Edwards' girlfriend, and he is sweetly making love to me for the very first time.

I can't wait to replicate the effort night after night.
I don't think it will ever get old.
Not with Bryson.
Not by a long shot.

Bryson

Damn.

Baya Brighton has the power to make me come on demand just from being in the same room, and now that I'm deep inside of her, I can't figure out how to make it last. She'll think I'm defective if I lose it before I get a single decent thrust in. And, with Baya around, I sort of am defective, in a crazy good way.

"Let me know if this hurts." I sweep a kiss over her lips. She's all but stopped breathing. Her hands are flattened against my chest as if she's getting ready to evict me. The inside of her body is so tight it feels like heaven, but I'm guessing it doesn't feel so hot for her right about now.

I pull up on my elbows and glide in and out, slow as humanly possible without turning this into a torture session for the both of us. Her legs relax and loosen around my back, so I take it as a green light and speed up a little.

"Shit," I hiss into her ear. "You're killing me, Baya." Swear to God it's never felt this fucking good. "I'm ready to lose it."

I give a few hearty thrusts the way I want to, the way I've been dying to right from the beginning. That first day I laid eyes on her, I wanted nothing more than to bend her over my mattress and thrust deep inside her until she screamed out in pleasure. I've thought about all the hundreds of ways I could have her, tossed off to her beautiful face regularly for weeks in the shower, but this was infinitely better than any fantasy, any convoluted idea conjured up by my subconscious. But I knew she wasn't that kind of a girl, no matter how hard her tits tried to convince me that first day, I knew she was sweet. That she was the one for me.

I reach down and give one of the girls a squeeze and lose it. Baya raises her hips to meet mine and digs her nails just below my waist until it burns in a fucking good way.

"Brys—"

I can feel her body jump beneath me, and I pray to God she's enjoying herself because I'm too lost in the assault to turn back now. My hips heave into hers until she bounces back into the headboard. I grab ahold of her shoulder and steady her beneath me until my body gives into a sweet release, and I shake over her in a cold sweat.

"Baya," I hiss into her lips before burying myself deep inside her.

She sighs beneath me, and I lay my weight over her for a second. I brush an apologetic kiss over her lips, slow and circular as I hike back up on my elbows. My dick starts to go soft, so I pull out and toss the condom onto the floor.

I roll back into her and study her beauty. Her smeared mascara, her full lips freshly glossed with her tongue.

"Did you like that?" I'm almost afraid to hear her answer. I've only slept with one other virgin and that ended with her screaming expletives at me as she ran out of the room. That pretty much crossed girls with no experience off my list, not that I had to cull anyone from the ready and willing pile. Turns out there weren't a whole lot of virgins at Whitney Briggs after all.

"Nope, I didn't like that." She pulls me in by the chin, and my heart drops into my gut. "I *loved* that." She runs her tongue over my lips like a promise of more to come.

My chest rattles at the thought. Baya didn't like it. She *loved* it. She didn't run screaming—I was her first, and if she'll let me, I'll be her last.

"Thank you," I whisper, pulling her bare bottom in the cleft of my stomach.

"For what?" She turns her head just enough for me to appreciate her beauty.

"For loving me." I press my lips into the back of her moist hair. "For letting me love you back."

ଛୀୠ

Late Sunday, we say goodbye to Mom and drive Annie back to school.

I take Baya out for coffee before we hit the Briggs Apartment building and make our way up.

"Maybe I should head back to Prescott and reclaim my dorm?" She squirms a moment, looking at the door as if it were her brother himself.

I hold up the hot pink giraffe we lugged home. "And what will we tell, Lucy?"

"Lucy?" She bats her lashes at me, and it takes all of the restraint in the universe not to kiss her. Oh, hell—I bend down and kiss her, long and strong, right here outside the door to our apartment, and I swear to God I can hear Cole sharpening the kitchen knives from inside. I pull back slowly, and my lips hold their puckered position a moment longer than necessary. "I thought she looked like a Lucy, but if you prefer Zelda we can negotiate." I give a crooked grin.

"Lucy it is." She takes the overstuffed giraffe and hugs her.

We head in, and, so far, the coast is clear, no sign of Cole or his many concubines.

Baya drops her bags on the floor and pulls a pen off the counter. She heads over to the scoreboard and pauses as she studies my side of the wall with a renewed interest.

"Whoa." I speed over but not before she adds a single tally mark toward the bottom. "You don't belong up there." I twist my lips at the sight.

"Oh, yes, I do. I *earned* my spot, and I won't let you take it away from me." She gives a little wink.

"Here." I swipe the pen from her and draw a heart around the line she inscribed. "We should at least get it right. I mean, you *are* the last."

"Really?" It comes from her weak, as if it were the last thing she expected.

"Yes, really." I brush my hands over her hips and brazenly steady her in front of me. "There's no one else for me but you, Baya. This is it," I whisper. "I'm all in."

She melts into me and wraps her arms around my neck. "I love you so much," she whispers with tears glittering in her eyes.

"I love you, too." I launch an all-out viral assault over her mouth as our teeth graze over one another, our tongues lash out with something just this side of anger. There's no way I'm going to be able to sleep at night knowing she's less than ten feet away in the next room. It's not right. She should be safe in my arms as often as possible and, for damn sure, at all hours of the night.

The door to Cole's room rattles, and Baya launches across the room like a missile. By the time I look over she's lounging on the couch reading a book—spinning it until its right side up. It's Cole's hunting and surviving in the wilderness manual—something that I'm going to need once he gets wind of what happened between his sister and me.

"You're back." Cole struts out, looking like hell, and I peer into his bedroom for evidence of a female suitor, but nothing. "You have fun? How's Annie?" He heads into the kitchen with his hair sticking up in the back, his body stuttering forward like he just got electrocuted. It's obvious he just woke up. Maybe he's slept through the weekend?

"Annie is great. Just dropped her off. We did nothing but watch lame chick flicks all weekend. How about you?"

"Chicks and flicks, just like you bro, but I did it a hell of a lot better." He plucks a beer from the fridge and pauses once he spots Baya. "Hey, kid, you're back, too."

Baya cuts a glance over to me. I can tell it frustrates her when he treats her like she's twelve. Of course, my body can attest to the fact she's all woman, perfectly functioning in every capacity, sweet as sugar in all the right spots, and now I'm hungry for more.

"Yeah, well, I've been here for a while. Thanks for noticing."

Cole tilts his head as if he's ready to call bullshit. He looks back at me and over to her as if he's doing the math, and I pretend not to notice.

Fuck.

"What the hell's that thing in the corner?" He nods over to Lucy, our overstuffed lovechild. "It looks like it's getting ready to attack."

Baya bites down over her lip as if she's holding back a laugh.

"I got lucky this weekend." She lets her words linger in the air, and I drink them down, enjoying the hell out them right to the dregs in front of her pompous brother of all people. "I won it in a raffle. I guess I can donate it if you hate it." She gives me a quick wink.

"No, it's fine." Cole seems pleased that Baya brought a toy to the apartment thus firming up his theory she's the mental equivalent of a thirteen-year-old. "It's kind of cute. Does it have a name?"

"Lucy." Her pink tongue twitches between her lips when she says it, and my dick perks to life, wagging in her direction—begging her to come out and play. If my dick had a mental age, it'd probably be about thirteen too, not that Baya is. She's miles ahead of me in that department. Why the hell can't Cole see her for the intelligent person she is? I really don't get it. It's not like I'm busy coddling Annie.

Cole takes a seat on the stool with a bowl of cereal under his chin as if it's always been there. "Aubree Vincent dropped by." He narrows his brows into her. Cole has the big brother intimidation factor down to a science. "She said they had a couple of dropouts last minute, and you were eligible to rush." He swallows hard. Cole looks hurt, vulnerable, and, for the life of me, I can't figure out why.

"Really?" She looks to me as she considers this. "Maybe I will." She glances back at her book. "Maybe I won't."

"Well, you can't stay here." Cole drinks down his milk from the side of the bowl. "You'll finish your back off sleeping on that thing, not to mention what you're doing to the couch."

"Gee, thanks." Baya pinches her lips to the side. "I guess if you really don't want me here, I can always go back to Jeanie."

"Speaking of Jeanie—I put a complaint in at the dorm." Cole gets up and dumps his bowl in the sink like it's no big deal and grabs another beer from the fridge.

"You *what*?" Baya jumps off the couch and springs over to his side, good and pissed. "What the hell did you do that for? She's going to hate me now."

"Relax." He darts around her and heads to the couch. "She doesn't even know who the hell you are. Besides, it's not cool that she's disrespecting you like that. Even *I* have the decency to shut the door." He raises his beer at me.

Baya boils over. "Cole, you can't just do things like that behind my back. I can fight my own battles."

"Oh yeah?" He bears into her stern as shit. "Then why are you here?"

Baya sucks in a breath that tells him to fuck off far better than words can.

"You're nothing but an asshole." She picks up her purse and storms out the door.

"Baya!" he shouts after her, but she's long gone. He looks over at me visibly pissed. "What?"

"Go easy, will you?"

"I can't dude." Cole blows a breath through his cheeks. "She's been lying to me."

"What do you mean she's been lying to you?" My gut flinches like I just got sucker punched.

"There was no fucking book club weekend getaway. When Aubree came and I told her where Baya went, she said she went over to the dorm because she wanted to drop in on them and tell her the good news herself. She came back in less than fifteen minutes to let me know there was no book club. She asked if she was seeing anyone—trying to insinuate that Baya was hiding some guy." He shakes his head.

Fucking Aubree. My blood pressure skyrockets as my adrenaline kicks in. She knew exactly where the hell Baya went, and she decided to start shit. A part of me wants to storm off and shake her, and, yet, the other part, the part that still has a foot in the past will never forget the day she looked me in the eye and said, *You did this— you took away my best friend.*

"Anyway"—Cole flops on the couch—"so, I went over to Prescott and found Jeanie bent over her desk with Stuart Saunders of all people."

Stuart was our third roommate a few years back before we found out he was helping himself to our wallets. He's damn lucky to still have air in his lungs, let alone the equipment necessary to bend Jeanie over.

"It's no surprise. That girl has always had bad taste." I snap a water bottle off the counter and take a seat across from him. "She slept with *you* didn't she?"

"You, too if I remember correctly—on multiple occasions. Anyway, turns out, Baya wasn't lying about Jeanie. I tried to see if they could pair her with a freshman, but Prescott's full. If she doesn't get into Alpha Chi, we'll be stuck with her the rest of the year."

I shake my head at the thought. Little does Cole know, I won't mind one bit.

I'm hoping to be "stuck" with Baya Brighton for the rest of my life.

7

Into the Fire

Baya

The sky above Whitney Briggs is a colorful palate of pinks and golds. Fall has come, full force, with the temperature dipping way past the sweater zone and into the cocoon-me-in-a-down-parka territory. I speed over to Prescott like I actually have someplace to go, and with each step it feels as if I've tucked a sandpaper tampon high up inside me—a half a dozen of them at least that have been soaked in kerosene and lit with a match. I was a little thankful when Bryson's mother shouted she was back from the other side of the door this morning. I used it as an excuse to hit the shower, but, truthfully, I don't think I could have stood another round of rock the cock without having medicated myself with a morphine drip first. I whimper a little because that's how its going to be in the future, me running from the sword dangling from his legs, and him trying to lure me back to the bedroom by way of higher power pharmaceuticals. I knew I'd be sore, but this was too unfathomable for me to have ever imagined. It's hard to believe other girls go through this all the time. I *want* to have sex with Bryson again, it's just that I'm not a big fan of having a blowtorch shoved up my nether region. And now I'm plain scared spitless to go there again.

Prescott comes up on my right, and I pause—too humiliated to step inside.

Freaking Cole. It's embarrassing to hear how he "handled" things for me while I was away. Who the hell cares that Jeanie Waters is trying to launch herself into Guinness by way of her love glove? I certainly don't give a flying fuck—and believe me I've seen her attempt "flying fucks"—it's *so* not pretty. Even Thing One and Thing Two looked terrified. Clearly they were unwilling participants in the failed acrobatics.

I head into Prescott and head up to Roxy's room hoping she's around.

The cat with its blunt F.U. greets me until the door finally opens revealing a puffy-faced rendition of Roxy that I hardly recognize.

"What happened?"

She lets me in and I spot Laney sitting on the bed, Indian style.

"Baya!" Laney jumps up and offers a quick hug. "Did you get laid?"

I scoff at her dime store description of what happened this weekend, but I won't indulge her with all the dirty details until I find out if Roxy is okay.

"More like rammed with a backhoe, but what the hell happened to you while I was gone?" I pluck a tissue off the desk and offer it to Roxy. The light from the window falls over her magenta highlights and makes her look even more gorgeous than she already is.

"Bad break up." Laney nods. "She's been dating Aiden Ryerson for the last three years. They like to break up now and again to keep things interesting."

I tick my head back a notch. I'm pretty sure no one signs up for that type of misery, at least not willingly.

"So, what happened?" I ask.

"Same thing as last time," Laney offers. "He *cheated.*"

"That's terrible!" I can't imagine how hurt I'd be if Bryson did that to me. Of course, I'd go into a psychotic rage at first and mutilate his reproductive organs, but I'm sure once I settled into prison life, I'd be pretty damn hurt.

Roxy takes a seat on the bed and starts to bawl. I lean in and rub her back while Laney rolls her eyes as if it were unrequited drama taking place.

"Don't bother feeling sorry for her." She makes a face. "Once a cheat always a cheat." Laney plucks at Roxy's arm until she's looking at her. "Don't waste this opportunity. This can be a totally empowering moment in your life if you let it. You need to embrace the pain. You should write this new skank a thank you note for finally opening your eyes to what an asshole this guy has been all along." Laney's curt demeanor is doing nothing to soften the blow, but I don't dare tell her.

"She's right," I whisper to Roxy while pulling back her heavy curtain of hair. "I bet there's a special guy out there just waiting to meet you. Someone who will love you with all his heart and soul." Last night comes back to me in snatches, and I cinch my legs together with a rush of pleasure. "He'll come to you at the right time." A vision of Bryson bounces through my mind as he trembled over me while my insides tore apart at the seams.

"And in the meantime?" She darts a look in my direction with her eyes like two red nests.

"I don't know." I glance around, and her laptop catches my attention. "Watch YouTube. You can log all kinds of insane hours watching kittens sleep and...Meerkat soaps—trust me Meerkats can be much better to spend time with than people." God—note to self: discover new ways to cheer friends the hell up without dragging poor defenseless mammals into the equation.

"Yes!" Laney bounces into Roxy. "I spent all day yesterday watching an entire season of *Downton Abbey*—of course it was a remake with Legos which only made it that much more fascinating."

Roxy and I just stare at her.

"Anyway"—Laney shakes her head—"I think we all know the only thing that will make you feel better is plotting a little revenge. We should hijack all his social networks and have him fess up to a violent crime."

"And that should land the feds at our door in about an hour," Roxy snarks. "No thanks. I'm not feeling up to any internet felonies today."

"Sunday is Halloween." Laney gets a crooked look in her eyes. "All kinds of freaky things go down that night."

"Again, no thanks." Roxy cuts her a death ray that says, *my cheating boyfriend lives to see another day.*

"So"—Laney clears her throat—"tell us about *your* weekend, Baya. Inquiring minds want to know all the dirty deets. *Dish.*" Her eyes widen. Her mouth hangs open, anticipating every juicy tidbit.

"We did it." I pump my shoulders like it was no big deal, but I can feel my cheeks filling with the fire from last night's lovemaking. There's no way those three little words could ever begin to describe what really happened.

"And?" She shakes her head unimpressed with my all-too-brief synopsis.

"Well?" Roxy leans into me, the patches on her face are already clearing.

"You really want to know?" If it'll help Roxy feel better, I don't see why not. I honestly don't think Bryson will mind.

Roxy and Laney both nod furtively as if I were the only person in this room to ever have sex. God—I'm not, am I?

Laney leans in. "We're like the only two girls on campus who haven't leaned on his crutch," she says it serious as death.

"First, that's absolutely disgusting, and, yet, alarmingly accurate. It turns out Bryson Edwards favorite team member is much longer than a crutch, and I've got the friction burns to prove it."

"Oh, that's totally normal," Roxy states, quickly regaining the even tone in her complexion. "I mean the burning—not the crutch."

"Really?" I'm mildly alarmed. "I love him and all, but I'm not sure I can handle this pain twenty-four seven. How do you live with this?" It's a wonder anyone has sex at all. Right about now I'm contemplating the miracle of life in an all new light. Women the world over must have some seriously high pain thresholds, either that, or we're *way* overeager to please our man.

"It goes away, genius." Laney swats me with a pillow. "And, if you do it enough, it never comes back. You were just too shiny and new. I'm sure his body will be a perfect fit over time."

Over time. I like the sound of that. And, yet, I suddenly wish we were past the Vicodin phase of our relationship.

"Well then"—I toss my hands in the air—"I guess I'll have to keep at it and let time heal this wound. Although, it'd better heal quickly, I'm not a fan of setting my kitty on fire."

They break out into cackles.

I fill them in on everything that went down at his house, Annie and his mom—the strange incident with the picture, and bumping into "her" brother. I give a stern look over to Laney because she damn well knows what I'm talking about.

"*So*—I gave you the 'deets' of my special night"—I say, looking right at her—"and now I want you to do the same. Who was she, and what the hell happened?" I glare over at her as a means of intimidation, but I get the feeling not too many people intimidate Laney.

"Her name was Stephanie. And I don't do people's dirty work for them. If Bryson wants you to know, he'll tell you." She shakes her head. "Look, Baya, I'm sorry. It's sort of a big deal. I really don't think it's my place to say anything. Just know that he's been self-medicating on any and every girl that would swivel her hips in his direction ever since he arrived at Whitney, but, now that you're here, he's hardly the same person."

"He called me his girlfriend." I shake my head, with tears pooling in my eyes because Bryson has something so frighteningly sad buried deep inside him, and he won't let me in. "I know it's silly, but it made me all kinds of happy."

"It's not silly." Roxy runs her fingers through my hair. "It's *beautiful*. And, it's nice to know that some guys still believe in the sanctity of a committed relationship."

That cheating boyfriend of hers clots up the air like some fornicating poltergeist.

I give a hard sniff. "Bryson is amazing." It comes out a little guiltier than I reasoned, considering I'm gushing over my boyfriend in front of a girl who was just brutally dumped by hers.

"Bryson *is* amazing." Laney touches her hand to my shoulder. "Just know that you're helping him heal, and, when he's ready, I'm sure he'll tell you everything."

When he's ready. It almost sounds cryptic. What if he's never ready? How long do I let such a big mystery linger between us?

Hopefully not long. In the meantime, I'd better double down on the ibuprofen. Something tells me this is the type of pain I'm going to come to appreciate.

ଚ୨୦ଓଓ

The week drifts by with Bryson and I stealing kisses while Cole showers—while Cole beds down an entire sorority house in his bedroom (no joke). Bryson and I take leisurely bike rides up to the Witch's Cauldron before class and hold each other while eating donuts and coffee, but we've yet to free my vagina of its inferno of pain by way of his curative friction. And, by the way, that doesn't even sound sane because it probably isn't even true. But, nevertheless, I'm up for another session of the lust and thrust, and Bryson Edwards is the only person on the planet I want thrusting anything in my direction.

I'm headed off to my music appreciation class, which isn't as easy as I thought it'd be, for one, there isn't a whole lot of appreciating going on as much as there is rabid memorization of classical snippets. I keep having to associate the music to different times in my life when it would actually suit the mood. Like, for instance, the time I was nine and I spotted my parents going at it in their bedroom. It was a trauma that left me bouncing all over the house in a panic because my brain didn't know how the heck to organize that clusterfuck of information. So, naturally, when I hear "The Flight of the Bumblebee," by Rimsky-Korsakov, it takes me back to that traumatic day.

A body slams into me on the main thoroughfare in the middle of campus, and I tumble back to find the bumble bitch herself—Alpha Chi's own—Aubree Vincent.

"Well, if it isn't little Baya Brighton." She wrinkles her nose at me like I just let off a foul sent. "Rumor has it you still want in. Is this true?"

"It's true." I swallow hard because it's sort of not, but maybe with me away from my brother, Bryson and I will be free to spend more time together—in my new bedroom.

"I talked to your brother this weekend." A thin-lipped smile glides across her face. Aubree would be beautiful if she didn't spackle a vat of foundation and adhere poor defenseless tarantulas to her eyelids for the hell of it.

"He mentioned it." God, I hope she's not planning on becoming his latest victim or, as it would more appropriately be—he would be hers. "So when's this alternative rush taking place? Can my friend Laney join?"

"Nope, just you. Be at the bridge Sunday at midnight, and come alone. Admitting members after rush is completely against the rules. I'm doing this as a personal favor because I just so happen to like you. But, if you so much as whisper to anyone where our secret meet and greet is, I *will* find out, and you'll be booted back to Prescott on your shiny white ass. Don't blow this." She breezes past me in her printed silk scarf, her long leather boots the color of honey.

"Wait!" I call after her. "Where's the bridge?"

"Figure it out," she shouts back.

Sunday. Why does Sunday sound familiar? Am I going somewhere, Sunday?

The picture of a ghost taped up on the window in Hallowed Grounds sends it all rushing back to me. Sunday—that's right, it's Halloween.

She wants me to meet her at midnight on Halloween?

Creepy.

I finally make it to class, but my mind keeps drifting back to Bryson and those electric kisses of his. I drop my pen three times, and the dark-haired boy in front of me is nice enough to return it each time.

"Thank you," I whisper.

"If I didn't know better, I'd think you were hitting on me." He gives a little smile. He seems sweet. Roxy should go for someone like him. "My name's Luke."

"Nice to meet you. And, by the way, you *don't* know better." I give a little smile. "Sorry."

He spins around, and my thoughts migrate back to Bryson and the bump and grind that played out for hours.

All I can think about is how beautiful it was last weekend. Bryson and I finally had a chance to be ourselves, and it only annunciates the fact that Cole has got to be dealt with. I'll recruit a pair of brass knuckles if necessary. It's becoming painfully obvious that Cole is the only one standing in our way of behaving like any other rational couple. And, once his mad cock blocking skills have been taken out, and he generously gives us the thumbs up, Bryson and I will be free to take our relationship public by peeing circles around one another in the quad. Of course, I'll make mine in the shape of a heart.

I let out a heated breath just thinking about what a task it's going to be to talk to my brother. I'll let him know I appreciate his efforts, but that he could kindly fuck the hell off because I'm pretty much going to date whoever the heck I feel like. Okay, so I'll be a little more gentle than that—a heck of a lot more gentle than that, but I need him to understand I'm more than just his little sister, I'm my own person. Also, I wouldn't mind addressing his tally mark addiction. He's beyond stupid for throwing everything away for a good time when there's a perfectly good girl out there waiting for him. Cole deserves to be loved just as much as Bryson does.

And if Bryson found someone special, so can my brother.

ॐ☪

I run my idea past Bryson that night at the Black Bear Saloon in between waiting tables.

"I don't know." His eyes enlarge the size of beer cans. "Look, let me talk to him first. Normally, I wouldn't

ADDISON MOORE

interfere, but I know Cole." He closes his eyes remorsefully as if he wished he didn't. "And, as much as he's your brother, I feel like he's my brother, too. This is going to gut him a little more than if I were just your average guy. He's going to think I betrayed him."

The music pulsates in and out around us. People from school have already started donning their Halloween costumes, albeit two nights early.

"Okay, but do it quick. I don't think I can handle too much more." I lean in and press my hand to his chest. "I miss you." I glance down at his Levis to get the message across loud and clear.

Bryson drops his towel and picks it up before spinning around like he didn't even hear me. A gentle tap lands over my shoulder, and I turn to find Cole and some beefed up linebacker next to him. That explains a lot.

"What's up, sis?" Cole gives a light sock to my arm. "Have you met Luke Carter?"

He looks vaguely familiar. He's got dark hair and incredible dimples. I can see why girls might drop to their knees in front of him, but, unfortunately for both Luke and Cole, I won't be one of them. All of my knee-dropping skills are reserved for Bryson.

"It's nice to meet you," I offer. "You guys want a table?" I point over to the back where most of the people from Whitney Briggs hang out.

"No, thanks." He slaps Luke over the shoulder then it comes back to me, Music Appreciation—Luke is the boy who's good at picking up pens and, apparently, girls. "I

236

thought maybe you and Luke could catch a movie or something. I feel bad that you haven't seen much of Hollow Brook. You in?"

Crap. Leave it to Cole to hand select a boyfriend for me. I'm sure he paid him not to touch the merchandise. Just the thought makes my blood boil.

"I'm working." I nail Cole with a look that says we'll talk later. "Or, trust me, I'd want to." I glare into my brother. "Because I am thoroughly ready to spread my wings." His face bleaches out. Okay, so maybe I could have chosen another analogy, but still, the premise is the same.

Bryson pops up and knuckle bumps Luke and Cole.

"What's going on?" He sharpens his gaze at my brother, and it feels like the temperature in the room just went up ten degrees.

"Baya and Luke were just about to hang out. You mind giving her the night off?"

Bryson's mouth opens as if he's about to say something, but he aborts the effort.

"Oh"—I widen my eyes at Bryson as if begging him to hoist me out of this verbal quicksand—"I'm not wearing anything decent." I look down at the shorts I swiped from Jeanie, my crop top, coupled with a pair of patent leather FMs. Surely my conservative brother wouldn't want me roaming the mean streets of Hollow Brook in what amounts to brothel-ware.

"I thought that might be the case, so I brought these." Cole holds up a bag, and I snatch it from him only to find my pink Whitney Briggs sweat suit staring back at me. Figures. Cole is still very much interested in me maintaining my V-card for another twenty years. Little does he know I turned it in last weekend to his beefcake BFF.

"Look"—I sigh into poor Luke who doesn't even realize his balls are on the line if he tries something with me—"I'm kind of not feeling that great. I really just want to finish my shift. I'm shy a few books for class, and I need the cash."

"*Baya.*" Cole pulls me to the side. "Why the hell didn't you tell me you needed money? You know that's what I'm here for. I want to help you in anyway I can." His eyes melt over mine with a layer of heartbreak underneath.

I cut a quick glance back at Luke. "I see what kind of help you're offering, and, by the way, *no* thank you. Do you honestly think I'm that desperate to have my brother hook me up? Don't you think I have what it takes to find someone on my own?"

Cole lets out a heated breath. His fingers fly through his hair in frustration.

"No, Baya"—he shakes his head good and pissed—"I'm afraid you *do* have what it takes to get a guy, *lots* of guys. I also know you lied through your teeth about where you went last weekend." His eyes remain over mine, and my stomach explodes in a ball of acid. Holy shit. Cole knows.

The air clots up in the room. The speakers blare some yodeling country song that mimics all of the disasters in my life, and I just want to crawl under a table and stay there while trying to avoid both Cole and old gum.

"I don't have to tell you everything." I practically spit the words in his face. "You're not Dad. You never were. You pretended you were, but you never came close."

"What's that supposed to mean?" His dark brows knit together. "I care about you. I don't want to see you get hurt by whoring around with a bunch of guys."

"Isn't *that* the pot calling the kettle black. I think you've perfected the fine art of 'whoring around,' or haven't you noticed the writing on the wall? I believe you're in the lead by almost fifty points. I hope to God your dick doesn't fall off, but, if it did, I wouldn't call it a loss. If you keep throwing yourself away like that, then you don't deserve to have one."

I hurry to the restroom, lock myself in a stall and just lose it.

Less than three minutes later Laney comes in, and I finally open the door.

"Sometimes big brothers suck." She pulls me into a strong embrace.

I don't think Cole will ever accept me being with anyone—let alone Bryson.

Cole's not at all like Dad.

He's a hypocrite of the highest order.

Bryson

Fucking Cole.

He's such an ass for treating Baya like she's still fifteen. He took off soon after their blowout, and, lucky for Luke, he took off not long after, too. I have nothing against the guy, but, if he thinks he's hitting on Baya, he's got another thing coming, namely my fist.

I watch as she and Laney wipe down the tables. It's a quarter to three, and you'd never know it by the way the co-eds still line the bar even though we shut down the kitchen an hour ago.

"Why don't you get going?" Holt smacks me on the ass with a dishrag.

"I should help you close." I watch as Baya frowns into Laney. Cole ruined her entire mood the second he showed up. It's obvious his opinion means a lot to her. I wonder if she'll have a change of heart about me once he fills her in on what a womanizing asshole I've been the entire time he's known me—not that she's completely unaware. It's just that hearing it from Cole might put some weight behind it.

"Don't worry about me, man." He nods over to Laney. "Me and Sawyer have got it handled." He steps in. "So, did you appreciate the big 'meltdown' last weekend?" His brows pitch so high they're about to rocket right off his forehead.

"I figured that was your doing." I shake my head. "Do me a favor, and don't go defrosting any more of our assets. I got this."

"Done. And next time a little thank you would be nice." His face grows serious. "Dude, I don't want to see you get hurt again. Got that?"

"Baya isn't going to hurt me."

"I'm not worried she's going to leave you. I'm worried you're going to do something stupid and leave *her*."

A couple of girls spill their margaritas, and Holt jumps on it.

I shake my head at the absurdity. I wouldn't leave Baya. There's no way in hell I'd let Cole push me around like some pussy.

Maybe I will take off.

"*Baya*." I nod her over, and she strides up with that sexier-than-hell smile expanding over her face. "You want to head home a little early and watch a movie?" I'm hoping she'll know what "movie" is code for because I can't take looking at her strut around the apartment in her skimpy shorts another second.

"Sure." Baya takes a step back and looks up at me from under her lashes. "You know what I really want to do, though?"

"I'm hoping." I hold back the shit-eating grin waiting to erupt on my face.

"This." Baya pulls me in by the cheeks and detonates a kiss over my lips that makes my balls ache with pleasure.

A series of *oohs* erupt, and a round of applause circles the vicinity. I know for damn sure that not one of those people are related to Baya in any way.

This is it. Baya is ready to take the next logical step and fill Cole in on our relationship. Now it's all up to me to man up and do it.

I hope to God I survive.

ॐ

Baya and I head back to the apartment because she's emotionally and physically drained.

Cole's door is sealed shut, but a steady stream of female laughter bleats from the other side. Figures. The fuck-fest continues.

I flip on the TV and find a movie we both agree on before we settle on opposite ends of the couch.

This sucks.

Baya and I just stare at each other while Cole and his girl of the night shout themselves into an erotic oblivion.

"You know"—she shakes her head as the climax subdues and all is quiet in the next room—"I don't see what we're so afraid of." She runs her tongue over the rim of her lip, and my dick perks to life.

"We're adults." I shrug as if it were no big deal.

Baya pushes her tits out in my direction as if she were offering them up for dessert. "I wish I had a nice mattress to lay on. This couch is really starting to mess with my back." The tiny dimple just shy of her lip goes off as she gives an impish grin. She touches her finger to her lips before plunging it into her mouth and pulling it out incredibly, achingly slow.

A hard groan comes from me, and I pull her up from the couch.

Baya latches onto me by the waist. Her fingers glide up the front of my shirt, and my stomach twitches as she runs her cool hand over it.

"I've got a really nice, comfortable mattress you can try out—I mean, if it's for your health you can have it." I swallow hard because I know for a fact we're about to cross one serious fucking line.

"Thank you," she says it while rolling her chest into mine, her seduction still in full effect. "But I really don't believe it's as good as you say it is." She runs her fingers through my hair, and my head rolls into her. "I might have to see for myself."

"By all means." I lead her by the hand to my bedroom and entomb us inside.

"So this is it?" She whispers looking around at the clusterfuck of clothes and books, my unmade bed that looks anything but enticing. Hell, I don't even know when I last changed the sheets. Maybe this isn't the greatest idea.

She reaches back to turn off the lights, and I stop her.

"I want to watch." I bury a smile in my cheek.

What the hell, she's already seen the mess.

"Well, then"—Baya drops to her knees and unbuttons my jeans—"I'd better give you something worth looking at."

"Baya," I whisper. "You don't have to do this."

"I want to." She works my jeans down past my knees and runs her cool fingers along the inside of my boxers until I groan. "You like that, don't you?" She bats her lashes at me. Baya tugs down my boxers, slow, like waiting for Christmas, and my hard-on pops out to greet her. "Wow, would you look at that?" She glances up at me. "No wonder it felt like a freight train backed into me— because it did."

Baya brushes her lips over me, and I resist the urge to thrust into her mouth. She bites down over the tip of my cock, and I let out a groan that goes on for miles. I didn't think I could get any harder, but it feels like I'm about to push right out of my skin.

Baya runs her tongue over the length of me then plunges over my dick with her mouth until it feels like she's deep-throating. I glance down to make sure she's okay, and she doesn't seem to be struggling. She rides her mouth over me in long, lean strokes, her teeth digging into me on the sides.

"Careful," I whisper, and she goes easy, washing over me with her tongue. "Oh fuck, yes." I want this feeling to last forever. Baya gets the hang of it, and my dick feels as though it's died and gone to some penile nirvana. I run my fingers through her dark hair and watch her steady motions as she rocks over me. It feels so fantastic that I'm about to lose it in record time. "Baya," I whisper, trying to coax her to pull away before I destroy this version of sexual activity for her, too.

A set of footsteps scurry down the hall. Voices bloom, then yelling, but I can't see straight because she's got me right at that magical place I've waited to be at all damn week.

"Baya, stop." I pull out just as the door explodes open, and Cole's wild eyes stare back at me with my dick in the air—his sister's lips ready to receive me.

Baya jumps up and screams, pushing her way past him.

Shit.

Cole thrashes me against the wall before I can pull up my pants.

"You *fucking* little asshole." He thunders in my ear. Cole sends his fist flying into my face, and I feel a pop in my lower jaw. He yanks me by the T-shirt, pulling me in nose to nose. "You said you wouldn't do that to my sister, man." His voice comes out hoarse like he's crying the words out. "And now you're screwing her right fucking next to me!"

The front door slams, and, for a second, I think it's Baya that's taken off, but she appears in the doorway, and my heart breaks for her.

"Get the hell off." I pull on my jeans with my boxers rolled in a knot at the base of my balls.

Cole stuffs his fist into my gut, and I double over trying to catch my breath.

"*Stop!*" Baya screams until it sounds like her lungs are going to launch across the room.

He knocks me to the floor, and his foot finds its way into my ass over and over while I cup my balls, trying to protect the things he's really after.

"*Cole!*" Baya claws at him from behind, but he lands his knee on my back and starts delivering hearty blows to the side of my face, my neck.

Shit.

From the corner of my eye, I see Cole jerk back, and Baya flies across the room.

"That's it." I leap up and snatch him by the throat. I pin his sorry ass to the wall and clock him a good one, square in the mouth, before his knee comes up to greet the boys.

"*Shit.*" I drop to the floor, and he gives a power kick to my chest.

"Stay the hell away from my sister," he roars.

Baya tries to make her way to comfort me, but he holds her back.

"You can forget about that asshole," he seethes into her. "This is the last time you'll be seeing him."

"Go to hell, Cole!" She tries to break the stronghold he's got on her. "*Bryson!*"

It takes all of my willpower to suck in a breath and stagger to my feet. The pain echoing in my balls is enough to land me into next week.

"Let go of me!" Baya screams, and a hard thump emits from the apartment next door.

Cole kicks me hard in the shin. "Get your stuff, and get the hell out," he thunders.

"I'm not going anywhere, dude."

He pulls Baya out of the room with him and slams the door behind them.

Fuck.

8

Caught in the Middle With You

Baya

"You're an asshole!" I scream at my brother at the top of my lungs.

More pounding ensues from the apartment next door, but I really don't give a shit if the entire building crumbles because of my outburst. I scan the area for something solid to throw and spot a beer bottle off in the corner.

"Baya, *no*," he shouts as I wield it like a machete.

"Well, I say, *yes*, for once."

He steps toward the television, and I hurl it, missing his face and hitting the screen instead. A large spider web of a crack stares back at me in its place, and I'm damned impressed.

"You fucking *broke* it." He straightens, pulling himself out of the moment. "Baya, come here." His voice softens. He's back to being his sweet self, and, to be honest, not a single part of me wants to be mad at this version of my brother. "Baya, I care about you. Trust me, the last person you want to be with is Bryson Edwards. The guy's a slime."

"No, he's not." I pull my hands over my hips. "Take it back. I really care about him, Cole. And, if you cared about me like you say you do, you would let me be with whoever I please."

"What the hell?" He says it mostly to himself, obviously shocked at the idea of me having my own opinion. "Baya, the guy is a jerk. He beds girls for fun. Look"—he walks me over to the scoreboard—"he keeps track of them on the wall like its some kind of game." His eyes bulge when he says it. He's so convincing, it frightens me.

"And whose score sheet is this?" I point to my brother's side of the wall, who, by the way, is blowing smoke in the face of the competition.

"He told you?" A guilty look crosses his face.

"Yes, he told me. We don't have any secrets."

"Really?" His brows pinch. His dimples depress. "So I suppose he told you all about Stephanie." His head ticks back a notch as if daring me to say it was true.

An entire dam of words gets locked in my throat.

"No." It comes from me in defeat. "He will though. When he's ready."

"So you don't know what's been eating at this guy for the last five years, turning him into some kind of sperm dispenser, but you're willing to get on your knees for him?"

I try to say something to defend Bryson—to defend *me*, but it feels as if an ex-girlfriend-shaped boulder has lodged in my throat. Tears start to come, and I snatch my bag off the floor and run out the door.

"Baya wait." Cole follows me down the stairwell, but my feet don't stop moving. We hit the cool night air, and I run all the way across the street back to Whitney Briggs where I should've been in the first place. "I'm not leaving you alone. It's four in the morning." The haze blows out of his mouth like steam as he pants alongside me. "You know I love you, right?"

I stop in my tracks and just stare at my brother a very long time as the sky brightens a pale shade of lavender. He has the same dark wavy hair, piercing green eyes as my father, same dimples, too and my heart breaks because not only do I miss my father, but I miss the old Cole, the one I thought I knew.

"No, I guess I don't know that you love me." I swallow hard. "I mean you always told me how to act, and who to spend my time with, but you've never used those words."

Cole pulls me in and sniffs hard into my hair. His chest rattles with grief. "I do love you, Baya." He pulls back, and the street lamp picks up the moisture in his eyes. "You're my baby sister, and I only want what's best for you." His voice cracks with grief. "You deserve some nice kid who's never even made it around the block, let alone entire neighborhoods. You're amazing, and I want you to have a safe, and wonderful life."

"You mean that?" I pull back as tears flood my vision.

"Of course, I mean that." He warms my shoulder with his hand. "Now come back to the apartment with me before we both freeze to death."

I hadn't even noticed he was standing here in nothing but his boxers. I glance back at the tall, glittering building with lights peppered throughout the facility.

"It's going to be awkward," I whisper.

"I'll leave him the hell alone, I swear. I just need to know you're not wandering around campus at this insane hour." He takes up my hand, and I let him. Cole walks me across the street and back into the warmth of the Briggs Apartment building.

"You know what I just realized?" I ask.

"What's that?" He holds open the elevator for me.

"That you haven't held my hand since I was nine."

Cole brings my hand up to his lips and presses a gentle kiss to the back.

"I guess what really guts me is I won't be the most important guy in your life."

"Cole." I pull him into a tight embrace as the elevator doors whoosh open. "You'll always be my favorite brother."

"I'm your only brother."

"Yeah, well"—I give a little smile—"that explains a lot."

We get out, and the door to the apartment sits ajar from our abrupt departure. We step in, and I stare toward

Bryson's room. I'm dying to go over to him. For all I know he could be bleeding to death no thanks to Cole and the foot loose moves he shoved into his gut.

"Will you check on him for me?" It comes out a whimper, and I lower my gaze because I have a feeling that might actually seal Bryson's death warrant.

Cole blows out a breath before glancing back down the hall.

"Nah." He flexes a short-lived smile. "Why don't you do it? I'm tapped."

"Really? You're okay with that?"

"Just don't do anything with him, please." His hands fly near his temples. "I'm not ready to go there. Not tonight."

"Got it."

"Baya?" He scratches at the back of his neck. "Where were you this weekend?"

Tears pool in my eyes once again because it kills me that I lied to him.

"I was with Bryson."

He gives a quick nod. "I never want you to feel like you can't tell me the truth again. You mean the world to me, Baya, and I was worried sick."

I pull Cole into another embrace. "You really are the world's best big brother, you know that?"

"I know."

"Hey," I blow it out in less than a whisper as I make my way back into Bryson's room. His head is buried under a pillow, and the lights are still on, so I turn them off and crawl into bed with him. "You okay?" I ride my hand carefully over his stomach.

"I'll live." He groans as he gets up on his elbow. The moonlight washes through the room and bleaches all the color out of our world. "Everything go okay?" He brushes the hair from my eyes, and the ghost of a smile plays on his lips. It would figure that he gets his boys handed to him on a stick, but it's me he's worried about. Bryson is just that sweet.

"Better than okay," I whisper. "By the way, I'm pretty sure he's taken killing you off his shortlist of things to do."

"My balls are glad to hear it." He dots my forehead with a kiss. "Come here." Bryson adjusts his pillow and covers us with a blanket from off the floor. "Does he know you're in here?" His strong hand traces along my thigh, and I lean further into him, encouraging him to trace out every nuance if he wanted.

"Yes, but he asked me not to do anything with you." I shrug.

"That's all right. He sort of disabled those services in me for a while anyway. I'm afraid he wiped out any children we might have wanted in the future."

"We'll always have Lucy." I snuggle into him giddy just thinking about a future with Bryson.

"We'll always have Lucy." He presses his lips to my forehead.

"Bryson?"

"Yeah?" He pulls me in until we're spooning, and his warm arm lies over my waist.

"Whatever happened to Stephanie?"

"I cost her everything."

"Will you ever tell me the whole story?"

"Yes, Baya," he says it sleepy with undertones of grief. His arm wraps tighter around my waist as if I were about to fly away. "I promise I will."

Bryson

I spend all day Saturday working my ass off at Capwell Inc. trying to get from under the plethora of files Aubree buried me in. I was going to drill her a new one for ratting Baya out to her brother, but since the shit already hit the fan, I thought why make things difficult for myself.

Aubree has made it a practice to accost me routinely ever since we were in high school. I'm sure she can't understand why I've bagged and tagged at least a dozen of her own sorority sisters, and yet I seem to be allergic to her blonde eminence every time she struts in the room. The problem with Aubree is that she would have never understood that she was just another get. She's the kind of girl who would want to stick around and be "the one," but I wasn't feeling it before, and now that I have Baya, for sure, I want nothing to do with Aubree. The truth is, before Baya I wasn't feeling it for anyone—not even Steph and that's the reason things went down in flames. But I'm feeling it now for sweet, beautiful Baya. I hope to God she doesn't hate me one day for trying to make it work with her.

"You're here bright eyed and bushy tailed." Aubree saunters into the office with her tits thrust forward, ass out. I swear, half the time she looks like a cartoon character. She comes in for a closer inspection of my scrapes and bruises. "Holy shit." She gives a little laugh. "Someone had a rough night. Care to talk about it?"

"Not particularly."

"Your little girlfriend show you who's boss?" It titters from her like the juiciest piece of gossip.

"Nope." I lean in my chair and throw my hands behind my neck, affording her the bird's eye view. "It was her brother."

Her mouth drops to her feet. "He really did a number on you." She sits on the edge of my desk, and I avert my eyes at the thought of her getting comfy. "So what happened? Dump the little slut so soon?"

"She's not a slut, don't call her that. And, no, I didn't dump her. We're still very much together."

"Hmm." She makes a face. "I talked to her last week, she still wants in at Alpha Chi."

I shake my head stymied by this. "She probably likes the idea of having girls around once in a while."

"You used to like that idea." Aubree bears into me with a razor sharp stare that threatens to finish the job Cole started.

"People change."

"Not usually." She walks out of the room with nothing but the clatter of heels.

ଞଠଔ

ADDISON MOORE

Late that afternoon I get home and find Baya sprawled on the couch, reading a magazine. Her dark hair floats around her like beautiful, exotic leaves. The rosy glow in her cheeks makes her look like an angel that just had the orgasm of a lifetime, and suddenly I want to be the one to give it to her, right here, right now.

"Hey, gorgeous," I say at the peril of my own balls. I have no clue where Cole is. "You want to go for a quick bike ride?"

Baya and I change and head out to our place, the Witch's Cauldron. I try to race her uphill, but she's panting pretty bad and struggling. I encourage her to get off the bike, and we walk them the rest of the way.

"You really are a nice guy." Her dimples press in, and it drives me wild. "Most people would have taken off and waved their victory in my face but not you. You're a perfect gentleman. I think you're a rare breed. Any girl would be lucky to have you in her life."

A pang of grief hits me when she says those last words. I know one girl who probably wishes she never knew me, but, then again, she's not alive to think or breathe or wish, and that dark cloud of grief settles over me again.

We hit the boulders then climb over into the small clearing where the water bubbles and brews.

"Tomorrow is Halloween." Baya licks her lips as if she were simply using the holiday as a means of seduction.

Baya could seduce me just by breathing the same air. Come to think of it, there's nothing about her that doesn't hold the ability to drive me insane.

She wraps both her arms around my waist. "Do you know what you're going to be?"

"I was thinking about a pencil, and maybe you could be the eraser." I give her ribs a quick squeeze, and she bucks beneath me.

"I'd never erase you." She holds back a smile while taking off her shoes and rolling up her jeans. "How about Bonnie and Clyde?" Baya sits on the lip of the spring and dips her feet into the water.

"How about Adam and Eve?" I ask, plucking off my sweatshirt. "We can get into costume right now." I keep stripping until she's standing next to me, amused. "I double dog dare you to join me."

Baya flicks her clothes off as if there were a swarm of bees nesting in them.

I pluck at the band of my boxers and pause. The icy autumn air swirls around me with its arctic blast.

"If you're going to do it, I think you should commit." Baya pulls them down until they slide off on their own.

"I think maybe you should consider doing the same." I give a crooked smile as I unhook her bra. I slip her panties past her waist, and she wriggles out of them. "Last one in is a rotten egg."

Baya slips by me, and glides in, slick as a ninja.

"No fair," I say, lowering myself into the boiling water. "Your brother disabled me last night." I melt into the spring, and the heat calms my aching muscles.

"Sorry about that." Baya moans into me with a sexier-than-hell grin plastered to her face. "Let me kiss all your boo-boos. I want to make everything better." She runs her fingers up my thigh nice and slow.

"Permission granted." I lift my arms and push my chest into hers. Baya presses smooth, easy kisses over my neck, my shoulders, the underbelly of my arm before bouncing back up to my lips. I sear my tongue over hers while digging my fingers into the back of her moist hair. "God, I love you." I pant over her ear while my hard-on nestles itself perfectly between her legs as if it belonged there, and I very much think it does.

Baya pulls back and examines me. Her lawn green eyes stand out against the backdrop of the storm clouds brewing up above.

"I love you, too, Bryson."

There's a sadness in her eyes that I've never seen before, and a part of me wants to ask if I've caused this grief—if this has anything to do with the fact I haven't opened up to her entirely—yet, deep, down I know it is. I'm almost ready to crack open the painful vault of the past and let Baya in, let her see the carnage I'm responsible for, and maybe that will explain why I wanted nothing to do with love, until now.

"I cleaned my room for you," I say, sheepishly. "If you want, you can take all the drawers, I don't need them.

I know Cole suggested we kept it chaste around him, so I'll take the couch."

Baya twists her lips a moment. "I might have a place to stay after the weekend. That way you and Cole can maintain your man-cave, and you won't get sick of having me around."

"Trust me, I will never tire of you, Baya." I spin her in the water. "I promise you this."

"That's funny"—she whispers the words over my cheek, and it cools me—"I feel the exact same way."

"I want to make love to you," I say it pleadingly into her eyes. "I want to do it over and over and over again, and then I'm probably going to fuck you just to round out the evening."

Baya belts out a laugh, and her voice rises to the top of the pines, before spiraling off to heaven.

"I double dog dare you." She tilts her head. Her lips look soft—red as cherries, so I lean in and take a quick bite.

I cup my hands over her soft tits and dip my head down until I'm covering her nipple with my mouth— exactly how I wanted to do it that first day in Founder's Square. My lips move up her neck, and I lick a line straight up to her ear before running my tongue inside it, and she squirms with a laugh. My mouth melts over her for a small eternity. I could easily spend hours doing just this. I roll my tongue over her and memorize the way she feels in my mouth, over my teeth.

I swipe another quick kiss off her lips, already lightheaded from Baya's special brand of magic. "Maybe I'll just fuck you right now," I whisper it low.

"Oh yeah?" She bats those long lashes at me, and my dick ticks under her. "I think you're all talk and no action, Edwards."

My head dips back as I give a dark laugh. "It's on, girl." I reach over to my jeans and dig out a condom. I've never put one on under water before, but I'm hoping it's just as useful as it is on dry land.

Baya watches as I submerge it and roll it over myself under the vaporous steam.

"It takes a talent," she muses.

"I've got plenty of talent." I give a devilish grin. "In fact, I'm about to show you just where my talent lies." I dip my hand between her thighs and rub my thumb over the softest part of her. My finger glides back slipping deep inside her, careful and slow.

Baya closes her eyes and lets out a breath. "Yes," she whispers, biting down on her strawberry-colored lip. "You are quite talented."

Baya wraps her legs around my waist and guides me in. I take it slow and easy, pushing in inch by inch, watching her face to see if I'm hurting her. I press her in by the small of her back, and she takes in a quick breath.

"Okay"—I glide out—"we don't have to do this." I might die, but that's not important.

"No, it's fine." Baya bats her lashes at me. "It didn't hurt at all, I swear. Besides, rumor has it, we have to do it"—she gives an impish grin—"a lot. And if we don't, my body starts from scratch." Her dimple goes off as if it were winking at me.

"That's one rumor I like."

"So put it back." Her eyes widen with the command. "Now."

"Damn, Baya." I give a little groan as I guide myself in again. "I think I like you large and in charge."

"Really?"

Her eyes glow a pretty lemon yellow, so I kiss each of her eyelids in turn.

"Really."

"Okay then, do that thing you said you were going to do." She lowers her gaze to my chest before raking her lips against it.

"Do what thing?" I think it's damn cute she can't bring herself to say it.

"You know." She looks up as the apples of her cheeks flame a soft pink.

"Say it, Baya," I whisper, grazing her thigh with my hard-on.

"Fuck me," she says it so low, I can barely make the words out.

"I'm sorry, I didn't hear you." I bite down gently over her earlobe and stretch it out with my teeth.

"I said, fuck me right now, Bryson Edwards." Baya giggles it out loud enough for her voice to carry up to the pines.

"Yes, ma'am." I land a wet kiss over her lips. "I follow orders."

Baya guides me in this time and presses into my back until I offer a full thrust. Her eyes flutter back, her mouth opens. It looks as if she's enjoying it, so I go with it. I reach down and cover her sensitive spot with my finger and bring her along for the ride. I wait until her breathing grows erratic, her eyes roll back into her skull, before I unleash and take us both to that special place that I swear has never felt so good before.

"I'm coming," I pant into her ear.

Baya clutches onto me. Her fingernails dig their way down my back and bury themselves just below my hips. A choking sound emits from her as her body trembles over mine, then I join her. The two of us lost in our love for one another.

I want to stretch this feeling out for all eternity with her.

It's magic like this with Baya, and I never want it to end.

9

Halloween Fright

Baya

Bryson Edwards is a god. No really. Sans that whole omniscient thing, he's perfect beyond universal comprehension.

The thought ricochets in my mind on a loop as I throw on my apron at the Black Bear Saloon. It's Halloween, and to say the freaks come out at night is putting it mildly. Tonight there's a freaks and Greeks invasion like no other. Girls in slut-ware, boys in...well, most of them are dressed as themselves.

Bryson winks at me from behind the counter, and my heart thumps as if begging me to jump him right here on the bar. He's got his five o'clock shadow giving him that sexier-than-all-holy-hell look, and his jaw keeps redefining itself as he gawks over at me in my bunny slash waitress uniform. Honestly, with the catcalls I got just walking through the door, I should seriously consider wearing this cottontail every night of the year.

Bryson, however, skipped the faux animal parts and decided to go rogue as a "bartender," an amply endowed bartender sporting some seriously hot tats, but, nevertheless, he and all his immeasurably long male parts are mine. I give a private smile over to him as he speeds this way.

"Nice ears." He swoops in for a kiss.

"You should see my tail," I counter.

"I plan on inspecting it in detail later tonight." He gives a naughty growl as his hands round over the back of my shorts. I've kept the summer wardrobe as a part of my work uniform because, let's face it, I get twice as many tips dressed as Jeanie Waters.

"*Hey.*" Holt barks over at us in his vampire attire. His face is covered with white pancake makeup while a trail of gelatinous blood drips down his chin. I'm not sure how he managed to do it, but he actually has fangs. "This is a family show. Keep your hands to yourselves." He gives a sly wink while conducting some major mixology behind the bar. "I'm teasing. Fornicate freely. In fact, I'd pay to see it. It's probably good for business." He holds up an electric blue drink for our approval.

"Nice," I say, inspecting the glowing concoction.

"You're gorgeous." Bryson leans in, and the sweet scent of his cologne intoxicates me. "I can't wait to get you alone tonight. I'm going to bite that tail off with my teeth."

"Mmm..." I give a kiss that pulls at his lips. "And I can't wait to get me some of those 3 a.m. kisses." I don't dare tell him I've got my haunted meet and greet with Aubree, the keeper of the Alpha Chi crypt. I've already arranged to borrow Laney's car for the midnight rendezvous. I made Laney swear not to breathe a word of this to anyone. The last thing I want to do is blow my chances at acquiring a room at the scholastic version of the Ritz. Besides, I'm sure whatever stupid Satanic ritual Aubree dreamed up won't take up an entire hour, and, then, I'll finally have a place of my own, free from overprotective brothers, not to mention the romping roommate I'll be leaving behind at Prescott Hall, although a small part of me will miss Thing One and Thing Two, perversely entertaining as they were.

Bryson turns to head back to the bar, and I land a brisk tap right over his rock hard ass.

"Meow," I purr over at him.

"A bunny that purrs like a kitten." He touches a finger to my long fuzzy ear. "Sounds like the best of both species."

"I'm just trying to lure you into the field so I can have my way with you." I run my finger down his chest nice and slow.

"Consider me lured." He tucks a quick kiss into my neck before heading to the bar.

I find Laney on the floor sporting the same cotton tail and ears which doesn't surprise me since we bought them together at the student store. I went over to her dorm earlier, and we drew cute little whiskers on each other and dotted our noses with blush, and she mentioned it was more action than she's had in almost a year.

"Guess who's seated at five o' clock?" She gives a quick glance past my shoulder.

"Five o' clock?" I'm the worst person to try and orient spatial relations by way of a timepiece. I glance over and spot a quasi-familiar dirty blonde dressed as a slutty farm girl with nine inch FM's and a dress three sizes too small. Her full lips siren out with bright red lipstick, and her nipples peer from her frilly bra every three seconds as she chortles herself into a laugh-gasm. Her suitor catches my attention, and I harden my gaze over at the boy seated across from her wearing a rather inglorious black cape. I recognize him instantly as the boy Cole tried to hook me up with. "Oh, it's that guy from my music class, Luke something. And why is this minute hand worthy information?"

"No, braniac—not him—the *girl*."

"The tramp trying to get her field plowed by the magician? Luke better get ready to let the ox out of the barn." The skank leans into him, and her boobs gyrate like bouncing balls. "Looks like the farmer's daughter is ready for that roll in the hay. You think we'll need security?"

"That's no costume." Laney slips a lock of dark hair behind her ear. "That's Jeanie Waters."

"*That's* Jeanie Waters?" I lean in to inspect her with the cosmetics-based disaster smeared over her features, the boob enhancing costume that's about to burst at the seams. God, I don't think I've ever seen her face. She was all hair and limbs, moans, lips, and penises coming out of every orifice. Her boobs wiggle again, and oh! It takes everything in me not to give a friendly wave over to Thing One and Thing Two. Here they were desperately trying to get my attention all along, and I was stupidly ignoring them.

Jeanie glances over at me and gives a sharp look.

"Shit." I spin abruptly. "Should I say something?" I clutch onto Laney and resist the urge to shake her. "Like—hello, I'm your invisible roommate! Would you please stop fucking over every free surface in our dorm room?"

Laney's eyes flutter. "It's subtle. I like that." She speeds me over to their table and drops me off with all the enthusiasm of a kid on the first day of kindergarten.

"Hi." I give a little wave at the two of them, but my attention gravitates to Thing One who has cleverly raised an eye at me and is bouncing away, happy to see me.

Luke peruses his menu. "Cheese chips, please."

"Oh" —I scramble to pull out my notepad—"right. Cheese chips. And for you?" I examine Jeanie in this close proximity. She looks like your average harmless skank, *nice* even, like she might say sorry after she gave you VD.

"Same." She waves me off and leans heavily into Luke as Thing One and Thing Two campaign shamelessly for his attention—by the way, Luke totally looks as if he's enjoying it. Figures. Typical perv. And Cole thought this guy was an upgrade from Bryson? As if.

"Excuse me?" Jeanie cuts me a look that spells *die bitch*. "Do you have a staring problem?"

"Oh, no. Actually—"

"Just get our food would you?" Her ruby red lips snarl up at me as if warning me to keep my girl parts from her potential sheet-shaking session.

Luke looks up at me, his eyes expanding with embarrassment.

"Um...I was going to introduce myself," I say, hesitantly as Thing One and Thing Two cheer me on with their incessant quivers. "I'm *Baya Brighton*." I enunciate carefully in an effort to talk over the music blaring from the speakers.

Jeanie leans back and glares at me as if I've just firmly lodged a knife in her horizontal hula plans for the evening.

"Well, *we* really don't. Give. A. Shit." She smacks Luke on the shoulder as she breaks out in a cackle.

"You know"—Luke shakes his head in disgust—"cancel my order, Baya." He stands and leans in. "Sorry about that." Luke takes off, leaving a horny as hell and just as pissed Jeanie Waters in his wake.

"Thanks a fucking lot." She stands toe to toe with me as if I might actually entertain the idea of a bar brawl with her and her quivering tits—and, for a moment, I do.

"Looks like the magician pulled a disappearing act." My lips give a wicked curl, and I don't stop them. "Anyway, I was just trying to tell you that *I'm* your roommate."

"At Prescott?" Her forehead breaks out in three narrow lines of confusion.

"Yes," I nod. "At *Prescott*."

Jeanie reaches to the next table and snatches the electric blue concoction Holt was working on earlier and thrusts it in my face. A small circle of gasps break out around us followed by a random round of applause while I blink and choke on the volatile brew.

"You *bitch*." I hold my arms out as the blue sugared goop drips down my fingers.

"That's what you get for reporting me to the housing authority." Thing One and Thing Two peek out from their frilly, lacy storehouse, surprised by this turn of events, because, clearly, I've offended them. "That was my *second* strike, by the way. One more and I'm out on my ass, and I'll be freaking homeless at Whitney Briggs." She stalks off for the exit.

"Join the club," I shout after her. "And I didn't say anything"—it comes out weak—"my brother did."

"Look at you." Laney appears and starts mopping up my chest with a dishrag. "Making new friends already." She dabs at my cleavage before making a face. "I think she dyed your skin blue. Oh, what the hell. It's Halloween. You could be a Smurf."

"Smurf." I sniff into the idea. "And she's the one worried about being homeless?" I shake my head incredulously as visions of her fornicating behind trashcans out in Founders Square blink through my mind. "Yeah, well, if I don't get into Alpha Chi, I'll be the one who's freaking homeless at Whitney Briggs." Well, not quite. I glance over at Bryson who seems to have thankfully missed the exchange due to the fact an entire gaggle of gorgeous girls have amassed around him. And sadly, tonight, we'll have to go into covert ops if we plan on shaking the sheets ourselves. Just the thought of getting it on with my brother in the next room is enough to kill my lady boner.

Crap.

I'm pretty sure whatever the pearl wearing, evening gown toting Aubree Vincent has planned for me to do this evening, I will. I'll leap through a thousand hoops of fire if I have to.

Like it or not, I'm Aubree's little bitch tonight.

Happy fucking Halloween.

ಹಜ

The moon hangs high over Hollow Brook like a silver scale as I drive Laney's sedan to "the bridge" just shy of midnight.

"Where the hell is the bridge, anyway?" I whisper. Laney gave me weird directions, but once she mentioned it was just past the Witch's Cauldron, I figured I could find it easily enough. She mentioned it was where Alpha Chi does all their bridging ceremonies. She also said she was secretly rooting for me *not* to get in—that too many oysters would be harmed if I did, per the mandatory pearl necklaces. She suggested I fashion Aubree's demon strand into a noose and hang her from the highest bough, what with no witnesses around and all, but I balked at the idea. Aubree's bitchy behavior is a small price to pay when crystal chandeliers and my own swanky sorority suite hang in the bounds. Plus, I don't mind pearls. It's not like they're going to force me to wear them twenty-four seven. I'm just thrilled I'll be living in a mini-mansion, far, far away from Jeanie and her never-ending bump and grind.

The Witch's Cauldron comes up on my right, and visions of Bryson and his magic fingers working me into a sexual fervor take over my senses. God. I roll my head from side to side. I can practically feel his lips branding themselves over my neck, his hard abs pushed tight against my body—that amazing feeling I get when he's high up inside me—well, other than the burning and the ripping.

I let out a breath as I park on the ridge behind the boulders. A dull smile plays on my lips. This is our spot. I can see the vapors emitting from the hot spring, and I'd like to think it's steaming up from the memory of the two of us writhing over one another in the tiny heated well.

I get out of the car and stare at the dusty trail. Laney said to follow it up the stream about five minutes, and that when I see Aubree's ugly face, I'll know I made it.

I take off on the dusty path lit up with the powder-soft glow of the moon and trek for what feels like miles in my patent leather FM's. It hadn't even occurred to me to bring a pair of flip-flops for the trip—or a sweater since it's cold enough to freeze the nipples right off my body.

The flicker of a candle glows up ahead, and I make out a suspension bridge that spans the length of the stream at its widest point. The water flows pretty wild, and every now again a wave hits the rocks and sprays me with the icy wash. The haze is markedly thicker up here.

The scent of night jasmine lights up my senses, and I take a deep breath just to trap the sweet fragrance in my lungs.

I spot a flame of blonde hair in the center of the bridge and wave.

The moon shines over a rusted out sign that reads, *Danger! Keep off.*

Figures. I bet wicked sorority sisters like Aubree are always looking to *up* the casket potential in any given situation, after all this is rush. Clearly a hazing of the acrobatic variety is about to take place.

I step onto the slatted bridge, and the entire length of it oscillates wildly. God, I hate these kinds of bridges. Once, when we were kids, we went on one at an amusement park, and Cole and a bunch of his bully friends waited until I got to the middle before jumping up and down on both ends. Assholes—assholes in *training* to be exact.

I grab ahold of the rope railing on the left and note it's missing on the right side. One good bounce and I'm guaranteed an ice bath. Great. I'll get to wash off the sticky blue liquid Jeanie christened me with by way of throwing my clothes over the rocks with my body still in them.

"Be careful," Aubree sings it like a taunt. "Take it slow. We have all night."

"Maybe you do," I whisper under my breath. But I've got some seriously hot kisses to collect in about three hours. If I'm lucky, and with Bryson I usually am, he'll have me purring until the sun comes up. I'm up for some delicious tricks and treats tonight, and not one of them concerns Aubree Vincent.

By some small miracle, I manage to hoof my way over, and not until I'm inches from her bare feet do I realize that I, too, could have taken off my shoes.

"Here I am." I hold out a hand victoriously.

"So you are." She smirks. "Did you come alone?"

"Just me, myself, and I." I wanted to say, *no Aubree. I have Bryson. Coming alone is what you do.* But I don't think she'd find it funny.

"Good." She darts a suspicious eye out to the black forest behind me.

"Did *you* come alone?" Somehow I find her need to trek out to the middle of nowhere suspicious and more than slightly creepy in a chainsaw massacre kind of way.

"Of course—" She bites down on her lip. "I didn't. I've got half a dozen sisters in the woods behind me. I need them to witness your pledge since you'll soon be a member of the most sought after sorority on the East Coast."

"Really?" My heart races. "So I'm in?"

"You're in." Her lips dig into her cheek just this side of a smile. "Repeat these words loud and clear. At Alpha Chi there is no me, there's just my sisters—the ultimate *we.*"

God, that's stupid. I repeat the chant at the top of my lungs like a private in the army, shouting it into the face of her overly zealous drill sergeant.

"Good. Now all you have to do is partake of the bonding libation." Aubree gleams a black smile as she plucks a small cup no bigger than a toothpaste cap from her fanny pack.

Fanny pack, huh? I would have expected something a little more chic from the queen of mean with a passion for uptight fashion, but, nonetheless, a luxury suite at Casa We-Chi waits for me at the end of this rainbow in the dark.

I peer into the tiny cup, and a gelatinous quiver stares back at me.

"Jell-O shots?" I balk at the midnight offering, but really I shouldn't. It's low-key compared to half the crap I would have easily agreed to. She clearly has no clue how much power she wields. She could have had me streaking across campus with leeches strategically placed over my body if she wanted.

"That's the last step, and you're in." The smile slides off her face as if that weren't the intent of the invitation after all. "Heard you had an exciting weekend with the Prescott Hall *book club*." Her lips curl in a snarl.

"Actually, I was with my boyfriend." I really don't give a shit if she knows. After all, Alpha Pee is all about honesty, right?

Her eyes harden over mine. "It must be nice to have finally nailed down the ever elusive Bryson Edwards."

Had I mentioned to her that I was seeing Bryson? Something about the way she says his name has me on edge.

"Let's get moving." She livens with a tiny smile. "This is the final initiation that every sister has to undergo." She pushes the tiny nightcap toward me, and I try to look impressed.

"So that's it? I down it, and I'm in? It's not loaded with blood is it?" Not that I'm opposed to drinking human plasma at midnight when my own private luxury suite is on the line. Plus, I'll never have to apologize to Thing One and Thing Two for ruining their chances with Luke Carter. In fact, I'll never have to look at Jeanie Waters' obnoxiously large nipples again.

"No, you nitwit, there's no blood in it." Her lips twitch. "Go ahead and knock it back. I've got places to be tonight."

I lick my lips a moment. Then it hits me. This is a *Jell-O shot*. "There's no alcohol in this, right?" I ask stupidly. Crap. I haven't had a sip of anything even remotely fermented after my father died, not a moment before either. Cole never felt that strongly about it to initiate some self-imposed alcohol ban, then again, I was younger when it happened. I was daddy's special girl.

"Of course, not. Do you think I'd waste some premium Grey Goose on a loser like you? Just swallow the thing so we can both get off this damn bridge."

"Did you just call me a loser?" I'd throw the cup in her face like Jeanie did to me earlier, but it wouldn't have the same effect.

"No I called you a *boozer*." She rolls her eyes. "Look, do you want the spot in Alpha Chi or not?"

"I guess." I run my tongue over the concoction, and the happy taste of artificially flavored strawberries greets me—not that I'd know what vodka tastes like.

"See?" She balks into me. "Just pinch it back. It practically glides down on its own. The sisters are waiting. If you don't do this, you can't get in."

I give the small cap a squeeze, and the concoction jumps down my throat as promised. I swallow hard, and it all goes down in one smooth lump.

"I did it," I marvel. And, it didn't taste like anything, so I don't really feel like I went back on my word not to inebriate myself at random. "So I guess we're done," I say, eyeing the dirt road from where I came, and the bridge splices in two for a moment. My arms and legs feel like they weigh a million pounds, and I'm suddenly exhausted beyond belief.

"I'd better go." She touches her pearls as if petting a kitten. "Say, you didn't happen to mention any of this to that hot boy-toy of yours, did you?"

"No." My tongue feels thick in my mouth—dry as cotton. "Bryson..." I start to say something then lose my train of thought.

"Yes, Bryson." She twists her lips "Want in on a little secret?" Aubree leans in, and her face expands and retracts as if I were looking in a funhouse mirror. "He gave me my first and last rejection ever." She wrinkles her nose. "Asshole, that one."

Excuse me? I meant to say it out loud, but my lips don't cooperate.

"I asked him to be my prom date way back when. Me asking him." She shakes her head and laughs. "Can you imagine? You'd think he'd be honored since he was just a measly little junior but, *no*, he was too far gone with that little brat Stephanie Jones. And she was about as annoying as you are. Anyhoo, I took care of that little bitch just like I'm about to take care of you."

She gives a firm shove into my chest and sends me backward into the icy cold stream.

My body seizes. My limbs refuse to move as the water washes over my face.

Can't breathe.

So cold.

So quiet.

The world fades to darkness.

Bryson

Holt and I watch, pissed as hell, while Jeanie Waters dances like a seasoned stripper on the slick granite of the bar.

"You know if she breaks her neck, she's going to fuck us sideways in court," I tell my brother. "Get her down."

The Black Bear is hopping tonight with every good little ghoul dressed for fornicating successes.

I keep scanning the place for signs of Baya. I've texted her twice, but she hasn't responded. Laney said she borrowed her car to do a quick change and come right back. I should have kicked Jeanie out as soon I heard she threw a drink in Baya's face.

Laney comes over looking visibly shaken.

"What's up?" I lean into her. "You get stiffed again?" It can be pretty tough sometimes to squeeze a tip from a drunken co-ed.

"No, it's not that." She snaps off her rabbit ears and stares down at them. "It's almost two-thirty. Baya left hours ago."

"I was thinking the same thing." My heart starts ticking like a bomb. "I'm going to take off and see if I can't find her."

"Wait," Laney calls after me. "She didn't go home to change."

"What?" Every muscle in my body goes numb.

"She's with Aubree at the bridge."

Holt pops up and swings a towel over his shoulder. "Who's with Aubree at the bridge?"

"Baya," I shout, rushing out the door. I jump in the truck, and Laney joins me.

A thousand thoughts swirl through my mind. Aubree said she'd let her rush. I bet that's what's happening. Maybe Baya got in a wreck on the way over? Maybe she hit her head, and she's passed out somewhere. Whatever the hell happened, it doesn't feel right. Something is definitely off. I can feel it in my bones.

"Text Holt and tell him to check out Alpha Chi," I bark into Laney.

I honk my way through a traffic light and bullet my way past the mansions where Alpha Chi nestles itself in the center of the opulent row.

I speed past a group of girls who just crossed the street as I head up to the main thoroughfare that leads to the bridge.

"I'm coming, baby," I whisper as I speed up the dark winding roads. I hope to God the only thing I find is Baya and a bunch of girls from Alpha Chi singing in a circle.

Somehow I doubt that.

ಹಿﾤದ

I race us over to Pike's Peak where the bridge is located. I'm shaking with frustration and pissed to hell just praying Baya is safe.

"That's it," I say as I spot Laney's sedan parked in front of the boulder where Baya and I have taken our bikes these past few weeks. The Witch's Cauldron sits just beyond it, and the bridge is a good ways up ahead. I jump out and am half way up the trail before I hear the door slam again.

"*Baya!*" I scream, navigating my way through the brush. I hit the bridge and jump onto it, giving it a mean sway, but there's nobody up here. "Shit." I dig my fingers into my hair. Baya is here somewhere. "I'm going to find you." I start making my way across the bridge and glance back to see if Laney has caught up yet, but a pale branch in the stream catches my attention, and I freeze in my tracks. That's no fucking tree limb. That's a leg.

Without thinking, I jump in.

"Baya!" I shout as I traverse a downed birch trunk to get to her, but she doesn't flinch. "*Fuck.*" I make my way over and pluck a dried shrub off her chest. Her head is perched on a rock close to shore, and her body is hugging a boulder preventing her from drifting downstream. I pick her up and place her lips to my cheek and feel a warm breeze expel as she breathes over me. "Baya." I pull her close as I climb us out of the rocky crag.

Laney comes up on us and lets out a viral scream.

"We got to get her to the hospital, *now*," I pant, racing back to the truck. "Baya," I whisper her name as I place her in the backseat with her head on Laney's lap.

I drive so fast that the road blurs through my tears. There's something startlingly familiar about this entire scene. It's all playing out like it did years ago on that fateful night that Stephanie died—getting a call just before dawn that Steph was in the hospital—finding out she hurt herself—that it was all because of me.

The hospital comes up on the right, and I barrel us into the lot. I park at the base of the E.R. and jump out, scooping Baya into my arms. Her lips are blue, her skin pale as chalk.

"Baby, wake up." I press my lips to hers as I hustle her to the front of the emergency room.

A woman with squatty features and square glasses points behind me. "Excuse me sir, there's a long line ahead of you."

"My girlfriend needs helps." A knot the size of a shoe lodges in my throat, and I can't get anything else out. "She's unconscious—she was in the stream," I muscle it out through the pain.

"I'll buzz you in."

I jet over to the entrance just as the door opens and lie Baya on the first gurney I see. A swarm of doctors and nurses rush at her and wheel her across the way, closing a curtain around her.

"Bryson." Laney pulls me into a hug and rains hot tears over my shoulder.

"She's going to be fine," I whisper. "She has to be."

"Bry!" Holt shouts from down the hall as he runs over.

"Where the hell is Aubree?" Laney clutches at her throat.

"I don't know," Holt pants out of breath. "But I found this."

He holds out a blue binder, and I snatch it from him. Written across the top in neat squared off handwriting is my name. "What the..." I open it up and find countless pictures of myself. Me in front of the Black Bear, the Sky Lab, my face in a newspaper clipping from my high school graduation. I flip the page and see my picture from the yearbook with my face X-ed out—devil horns drawn onto my head with fangs dripping from my lips. "Shit." I turn the page and freeze.

It's a newspaper clipping of Stephanie's obituary.

"Oh my, God," it stilts out of me in less than a whisper. It's all happening again, only now I'm wondering if Aubree had her foot in both disasters. She was Steph's best friend. She told me herself she hated seeing us together.

Fuck.

Hours drift by while an entire team of medical professionals work on Baya before they finally call us back. Cole joins Laney and me as we head in to see her.

There she is. Baya lies helpless with tubes and wires coming out at every angle—her beautiful face scratched along one side with a giant red welt.

"She okay?" I ask the doctor, staggering toward her.

"She's fine. Just a few scrapes and bruises on the outside." He sighs as if the worst is yet to come. "She has a small contusion to the back of her head. We pumped her stomach. There was a high dose of benzodiazepine in her system. It's similar to an extreme dose of valium."

"That's a fucking roofie." Cole's eyes are on fire.

The doctor nods and proceeds to tell us she'll be fine in the morning, but they'll need to keep an eye on her and might ask her some questions when she comes to.

"It was Aubree," Laney seethes as the doctor leaves the room. "That stupid bitch." She lets out a frustrated breath. "I knew—I *knew* I should have gone with her, but Aubree made her promise to go alone, and she was too afraid to risk it."

"That's Baya for you." Cole takes a step into his sister and gingerly picks up her hand. He leans in to kiss her and stains her yellow gown with tears. "She's used to doing what she's told."

I run my fingers through my hair as I go over and press a kiss to her cheek. "Baya."

"You think someone slipped it to her at the bar?" Cole looks over at me as if it were a possibility.

"No." An entire wall of words demand to break loose from my throat. I tell him about the notebook Holt found in Aubree's room, about her seemingly innocent obsession with me since high school.

"We need to call the police," Laney's voice shakes as she says it.

Cole holds up his phone. "Already did."

ಬಿ‍ಲ

In the morning, I rouse to a kick in the face by way of Cole's shoe. We slept head to toe on a crappy cot the hospital provided, even though we promised the staff only one of us would stick around last night.

"Dude." I nudge him away before leaping to my feet to see how Baya is doing. The cops let Aubree go last night because there was no evidence she slipped Baya anything. They said she could have gotten the roofie from the bar. I tried shoving the notebook up their ass, but they said Aubree was a third-rate stalker at best.

Baya is still asleep. They've already removed her breathing tubes, and the welt on her face has significantly gone down. The doctor said she was lucky she didn't slice her head open when she fell. The rocks in the stream are sharp as razors.

"Someone was looking after you, that's for sure." I touch my lips to her cheek. I'd like to think it was her father or Steph. That Steph really didn't hate me. That she cared about the people I loved and wanted them safe, too.

Her lids flutter.

"*Baya*," I pick up her hand as her eyes struggle to open.

Cole pops up beside me and shakes her shoulder. "Baya, wake up."

"Enough." I flick him off. "Give her some space."

"Bry," she whispers. Her lips curve into a smile. Baya takes in a deep breath, and her eyes spring open. "Cole." She looks right at him, and her eyes swell with tears.

"Baya," Cole leans in and kisses her forehead. "You're okay."

"What happened?" She glances around, startled. "Where am I?"

"You're at the hospital." Cole glances at me for support.

"You were with Aubree, last night," I say. "Do you remember anything?"

"That's right." She squeezes her eyes shut. "The bridge—the Jell-O."

"Jell-O?" I look to Cole a second. "Was it a Jell-O shot?"

Baya nods. "She said there wasn't anything in it but water." She shakes her head while struggling to sit up. "Obviously I can't hold my liquor."

"Why would you take anything from her?" Cole leans in as if he's about to reprimand her.

"She said I would get in if I drank it. She said all the sisters did it." Baya pushes out a breath. "I'm so stupid."

"I don't think you're stupid, Baya." I warm her arm with my hand. "Aubree has a way of making people do things they normally wouldn't do."

Baya looks up at me, the expression melting from her face. "So you know?" She nods as if I should acknowledge this. "You know what she did to Stephanie?" Her forehead creases with concern.

"What who did to Stephanie?" My heart thumps in my chest because it knows the hatchet is about to fall.

"Wait." Baya winces as she sits up. "I'm confused. I don't want to say anything. I probably imagined the entire conversation." She drills those emerald eyes into mine. "Bryson, what happened to Stephanie, and who was she?"

I take a breath and dart a quick glance over to Cole. I told him everything during a beer bender one night and have regretted it ever since. Steph was a wound I preferred to keep buried in the past—until now.

"She was a good friend of mine—my best friend. Once our hormones kicked in, we thought we'd give dating a shot, and that didn't work out so well. We tried to keep it together through our sophomore and junior years of high school." I swallow hard because I hate the next part of the story. "We were in the process of breaking up when she"—I take a breath and blow it through my cheeks—"she fell from a cliff." The tears come without warning, and I try to sniff them back. "The note they found said I was to blame."

Cole steps over and slaps my shoulder. "You didn't do anything wrong."

"Then why do I feel like shit?" I wipe my eyes with the back of my arm. "We had already broke it off about six different times. We were just kids. We were always fighting. I honestly thought we were about to get back together when she said she was coming to see me. Only, she never made it."

"Did Aubree know her?" Baya looks from me to Cole for answers.

"She was her 'big sister,' some program they ran through school. Aubree was always getting in our business. Why? What did she say?"

Baya's eyes widen as she fixes her gaze on some unknown horizon. "She said, I took care of that little bitch just like I'm about to take care of you—then she gave me a push."

The world freezes. The air in the room stops up, strong as death. Steph and Aubree used to go to the cliff to hang out. Steph said it was peaceful, that it helped center her.

"Shit." It bellows from my lungs so loud the walls shake with the echo.

It all happens in a blur—the cops coming in—Baya's mother storming the room once her plane touched down. Baya gives a firm account of what happened to her at the bridge last night, and the cops agree to call Aubree into questioning again.

They're reopening Stephanie's case.

Reopening the wound.

Hopefully, this time, we'll get some real closure out of it.

Eternal Love

Baya

The sky above the Hollow Brook cemetery is washed a creamy butter yellow. Bryson leads us over the polished granite stones as we tread carefully across people long since deceased in our warm wool coats, our winter boots.

It's been two full weeks since the incident, and I've got all my strength back. Aubree is being held on suspicion of manslaughter. Her parent's have already bailed her out, and rumor has it her father hired the best defense attorney that money can buy.

"Sorry"—Bryson apologizes as we skip over endless grave markers—"it's been years. At first I tried to come all the time, but her mom asked me not to. She wanted me to remember the happy times, and all this place ever did was depress the hell out of me."

I give his hand a firm squeeze because sometimes there are no words.

"Right here." Bryson nods into a large black slab of granite that reads *Stephanie Nicole Jones, Loving daughter and sister. Gone too soon.*

I hand him the bouquet of flowers we picked up on the way over—a fall arrangement with miniature pumpkins and fat orange leaves woven throughout a dozen yellow roses. Bryson said that yellow was a symbol of friendship—that they were never too serious, just best friends who tried to cross the line.

He lays the flowers over the stone before pulling a piece of paper from his pocket.

"I never thought you wrote this," he whispers it to the soil as if she could hear.

"Can I ask what it is?" I kneel down next to him as the iced breeze licks my ankles.

"A copy of her supposed suicide note. Both her Mom and brother tried to tell me it wasn't her handwriting, but I believed every damn word."

"Aubree did it." The handwriting analyst hired by the state already confirmed this. "Why bring a copy down here? I don't get it."

Bryson pulls out a lighter. "So I can do this." He sets the tip on fire, and it dissolves within seconds under the supervision of the flames. "Rest in peace, Steph. I knew in my heart you would never do it—never say those things. I'm sorry, girl. You were a good friend. You'll always have a piece of me. I hope you don't mind I brought along someone special today. Baya stole my heart." He glances up at me with his eyes glittering with moisture. "I'm in forever if she'll have me that long."

I lean in with hot tears rolling down my cheeks. "I'll love you for all eternity, Bryson Edwards. Nothing will ever change that."

Bryson smiles through his sadness just like he did that first day we met, but this time his smile expands, and I can see the downright joy in his eyes. He pulls me up, and we walk back to the truck. He wraps his arms around me and kisses the side of my cheek. I pause to soak in the beauty and the heartache of this afternoon.

"I'm proud of you," I whisper. "You're finally free of all that pain. You're a good person—you deserve to be happy."

"I love you, Baya." I can feel his heart pound over my chest. He pulls back and looks at me with those smiling, silver eyes. "Now and forever."

He crashes his lips against mine, and we indulge in a sweet kiss that seals our past, our present, and our future.

We're about to carve a new path in life—one that is built for two.

ಬೋಲ

A week drifts by, and I make my way across campus to my last class of the day. It's already starting to get dark out, and it's hardly three-thirty. A boil of storm clouds sift overhead, and if it gets any colder, Bryson said it might snow. My entire person tingles just thinking about him—about what a fun time we're going to have this weekend.

He invited Cole and me to spend Thanksgiving with his family.

"Baya!"

I spin around to find Laney and Roxy waving to me from outside the Hallowed Grounds café. It's freezing out, but they've installed outdoor heaters that look as if they could melt all of Prescott Hall if they wanted. I head in that direction and grab a seat.

Roxy has her hair splayed out over her trench coat, and she looks like a porcelain doll, she's literally that perfect. Laney pushes a cup of coffee at me, and I take a quick sip to heat my frozen bones.

"We're celebrating!" She stretches to the sky with a victorious gleam in her eye.

"You got the part? You're Whitney Briggs' new Fantine!" I catch a breath as if I were about to star in Les Mis myself.

"Better. You're looking at the new Madame Thenardier." She touches her fingers to her chest and mock bows.

"Yeah"—Roxy pushes into her playfully—"the feisty keeper of the inn. You'll really have to dig deep to channel your inner sarcastic bitch."

"You think you're funny, don't you?" Laney cuts her a look before reverting her attention back to me. "Speaking of news—we've got some for *you*." Laney tucks a sly smile in her cheek.

"About Aubree?" I'm still waiting to hear anything at all about her conviction. Personally, she still scares the hell out of me.

"Nope." Laney spins her cup with a devious look in her eye. "Actually it has to do with Jeanie Waters."

I suck in a breath. "God, did Aubree try to off her, too?" I can just imagine Thing One and Thing two quivering with fear.

"No." Laney ticks her head back, and her dark glossy waves bounce around her face. "My roommate, Amanda Ester, agreed to room with her. And, now, I have a free bed. It's yours if you want it."

"Oh." I pull a bleak smile. "Trust me, one week with Jeanie, and your roommate will be back."

"Not true." She holds up a finger. "I have enough dirt on Mandy to send her packing to the Alps if I wanted."

"So it's really mine?"

"It's really yours."

"Wow, thank you!" I lunge over and give her a big rocking hug.

"That's great for you guys." Roxy sets her lips in a pout. "I wish I could bunk with you. My roommate snores like she's blowing bubbles under water all night. I swear I can't get a wink in. Anyway, it doesn't matter. What I really need is a place with a bona fide oven. There's a big baking contest coming up—with a ten thousand dollar award on the line."

"You wouldn't think she needed the cash." Laney rolls her eyes into me. "Her father owns half the country."

Roxy nods. "My dad is a firm believer in me making my own way in the world. He's paying for school, then I'm on my own."

"She can't even squeeze an oven out of his tight ass." Laney shakes her head.

Roxy sighs into this sad reality. "Anyway, there's an apprenticeship awarded to the winner at the Sticky Quickie bakery. And, I know for a fact, the owner is a master baker. This could be big for me. Especially since I plan on opening my own shop one day. I know I can ace this, I just need somewhere to bake a damn cupcake."

"How about the caf?" Laney tightens her coat around her as the wind picks up.

"They gave me a big fat no."

"Sorry to hear that," I say. Poor Roxy. It's the last thing she needed after nursing a broken heart all semester. "How are things going, you know..." I bite down over my lip half-afraid to finish the thought.

"With my love life? I've been eating a lot of forbidden sweets—translation I'm on the cupcake diet, and it sucks because I can't even make the damn things myself."

"Cupcake therapy can only get you so far." Laney pushes into her shoulder so hard she just about knocks her off the chair. "You got to get back out there."

"No way. I'm swearing off boys for a good long while. They're pigs—every last one of them." She thumps her cup against the table as if to annunciate her point.

"Well, maybe not Bryson. You got sort of lucky with that one."

Definitely not Bryson. "Sometimes you just have to take a risk." Sort of the way my boobs did that first day in Founder's Square. I blush at the thought. "Hey, there's a party at the Black Bear tonight. Rumor has it all the hottest boys in the tri-campus area will be there."

"So soon after I've sworn off penis slingers?" Roxy mocks my attempt to get her mind off a boy by way of more boys.

Laney leans in as if to coax her. "Plus, Baya and me." She blinks a smile.

"I'm in." She raises her coffee. "To hot boys, who I *still* want no part of."

"To hot boys," Laney and I say in unison.

Only, Laney doesn't seem that convinced either.

It looks as if I'm the only one lucky in love around here. I have Bryson Edwards—and that really does make me the lucky one.

Bryson

Bodies bump and grind at the Black Bear Saloon as an endless stream of people filter in, but it's Baya I'm waiting for. I've had great news to share with her all day, and I wanted to do it in person.

"Dude," Holt moans. "How many times do I have to tell you, we don't need to run happy hour all night on weekdays."

"Just Wednesdays," I correct. "Besides, it's hump day. It's a perfect fit."

"Oh really? Because this is what you get." He shakes his head into the boisterous crowd.

"Can't you look on the bright side? Pretend each one of these people has a dollar sign on their face. That ought to take the edge off the misery."

"They suddenly look better."

"Thought so."

"Damn, they're attractive," he smears it with sarcasm. "You know we're about to break fire code."

"Relax, we're not there yet."

Cole struts up and knuckle bumps the two of us. We haven't spoken since the incident. Not that I hadn't tried to start up a conversation or two, he just simply left the room whenever I opened my mouth.

"You giving beer away again?" He nods over to Holt.

"That's probably my brother's genius plan for Thursdays," Holt smirks, handing him a tall amber bottle. "I was just telling him we're pushing the fire code."

"Dude." Cole slaps me over the shoulder. His eyes settle on mine, filled with a mixture of desperation and hurt. "Baya's my sister. You know what that means right?"

I swallow hard because I'm pretty sure it means I lose my balls in some inglorious manner.

He closes his eyes a moment. "It means you'd better take care of her, or I'm coming after you hard. She means everything to me, and if you break her heart, I'm going to have to break your balls."

"Got it." A barely-there smile starts on my lips as I resume my normally-scheduled breathing. "I'm not hurting Baya, ever. She's got my heart. All of it."

Cole tweaks his brows before doing a double take at the door.

"Five alarm redhead, coming this way." He slides his drink toward Holt as if disowning it.

I glance back to see Baya and Laney with Roxy Capwell.

Baya comes in and slips her arms around my waist, giving me that sweet smile I've waited all day to appreciate. I land my lips over hers and a hard swat lands over my shoulder.

"Dude, try not to manhandle my sister." Cole looks resigned to the fact we're going to ignore him.

Baya glances up at the ceiling. "Laney, Roxy, please find a pool of sorority girls and throw my brother in."

"Not so fast." Laney gets a wicked gleam in her eye. "Cole have you met Roxy Capwell?"

Roxy rolls her eyes at Laney's attempt at matchmaking.

"Cole Brighton." My womanizing ex-roommate steps in and takes up her hand, which reminds me.

I pull Baya in and drop a kiss on her forehead. "You mind if I steal you away a minute?"

"I double dog dare you." There's a sexy as hell gleam in her eye that I'm accepting as a proposition.

I pull her behind the counter a moment. "I found a room for you." A shit-eating grin struggles to break free, but I won't give it.

"Really?" Her brows flex just the way I've seen Cole's do a million times. "You're too sweet, but Laney beat you to it. I'll be rooming with her at Prescott. She blackmailed her old roommate into bunking with Jeanie."

Crap. I blink a smile.

"So where's the room?" She hikes her shoulders to her neck. "Let me guess. Alpha Chi wants to thank us for taking down the wicked witch of the East, and they've demanded I become their fearless leader?"

"Not quite." I twist my lips as I pull her in close. "The guy next door moved to a different floor, so I took up the vacancy."

"You're going to be Cole's neighbor?" Her eyes widen with a hint of confusion.

"And, if I'm lucky, so will you," I say with apprehension.

Baya's mouth falls open, her gaze shifts back to her brother.

"It's okay," it speeds out of me. "You can say no. I totally get it. Living with someone is a huge step—but, for the record, this is a two bedroom. I was sort of gunning for the hottest roommate in town."

Her lips curve in a delicious smile. "Just town?"

"The universe." I plant a kiss over her cotton soft mouth and linger. "But don't worry about the room. I can always find some dude who hates hygiene as much as your brother."

"Whoa." She lays her hands over my chest. "Who says you can give away my room?"

My heart gives a quick thump. "You're okay with it?"

"Of course I'm okay with it. As long as I have my own room, we can still maintain an air of mystery to our relationship."

"Mystery—I get it." I don't, but, then, I'm not smart enough to understand women. A burst of adrenaline rockets through my veins, and I pick Baya up and spin her around.

"Will you save a spot for me on your bed?" She bats her amazingly long lashes at me, and my dick perks to life.

"It's yours as often as you want it."

"I'll only want it on days that end in Y."

"Damn. You know how to get me going girl." I land my lips over hers and sink a kiss into her strong enough to fuel rocket ships. This is perfect love, something eternal.

Baya and I made our way to one another in this crazy world, and, in a strange way, it was because of Steph.

I pull back and admire Baya's beauty under the spotlight just above the bar. "You know"—I press my lips together a moment—"I never told you this, but that day I bumped into you in Founder's Square it was Steph's birthday."

Baya's fingers fly to her lips. "Oh my, gosh—I don't know what to say. I'm so sorry."

"Don't be." I press into her. "I was wandering aimlessly, and I remember thinking, I wonder what she would want me to be doing and with who—that's when you flashed me."

Baya's face ignites a like a blowtorch.

"Really?" She blinks back tears. "You don't think..." Baya bites down on her lip.

"I'd like to." I give a sheepish grin. "She was always looking out for me. She wanted me to have the best. And I got you, didn't I?"

"You're amazing, you know that?" She rides her finger down my chest, and my gut cinches. "And, you're also my new roommate, which means I have to apologize until I'm blue in the face to Laney."

"About?" Laney comes around the counter to grab an apron with Roxy in tow.

"You just lost your roommate again. I've had a hotter proposition." She bats her lashes into the girls. "Bryson took the apartment next to Cole's."

"What about me?" Cole comes up and thumps me in the chest. "Who's going to cook and clean around the place with you gone?"

"Did you say, cook?" Roxy's face lights up.

"Yeah." Cole smacks me in the arm. "I had him whipping up five course meals and hand washing my boxers."

Roxy narrows in on Cole. "I'm not cooking anyone a five course meal, and I promise I will *never* touch your boxers, but, if you'll consider me, I can keep you in cupcakes."

You can practically see Cole's hard-on screaming, hell, yes.

"I like cupcakes." He lowers his lids as if he's luring her to the bedroom.

"Cool." Roxy hikes her shoulder in his direction. "And don't expect anything else."

They take off into the shuffle of bodies, leaving me with Baya in my arms.

"It looks like it's just me and you." I hold her gaze stronger than steel. "I took a risk with my heart, and it paid off. Thank you for that."

"Bryson," she whispers. "I love you insanely, you know that?" Baya jumps up and wraps her legs around my waist. "You know what I'm going to love the most about working with you—*living* with you?"

"Watching me walk around in my underwear?" I deadpan.

She wrinkles her nose and looks cuter than hell in the process.

"What? It's the new dress code for bartenders." I firm my grip under her thighs. "And I'm instating an apron-only dress code for you."

"Just me?"

"Yes, but it's limited to the apartment."

"Very funny." She tilts into me, her dimples cinch up on the sides, and my stomach bottoms out because she's all mine. I'm the lucky one who gets to spend forever with her. "You know what I'm looking forward to the most?" She gives my waist a firm squeeze.

"Just hanging out—free to be you and me?"

"That, and those amazing 3 a.m. kisses."

"To 3 a.m. kisses." I lean in and brand my lips over hers. Baya tastes like strawberries dipped in sugar and every good dream I've ever had rolled into one.

"You know what I think we should do tonight after closing?" She gets a devious look in her eye, and, already, I like where this is headed. "Each other. On the bar."

An approving groan rips from my chest. Forever isn't going to be long enough for me to love Baya. "I double dog dare you."

Thank you for reading, **3:AM Kisses.** If you enjoyed this book, please consider leaving a review at your point of purchase.

Look for **Winter Kisses** (3:AM Kisses Book 2) Laney and Ryder's story, now available. **Sugar Kisses** (3:AM Kisses Book 3) Roxy and Cole's story, now available. **Whiskey Kisses** (3:AM Kisses Book 4) Holt's story available May 2014.

Acknowledgments

I can't even begin to thank everyone I need to for helping me with this book. My family has been my rock through every step of the way, and I'll never be able to repay you enough for doing the dishes, helping with dinner, and, on those few occasions in which I do cook, for pretending to like it. We should go out sometime. Oh, and that whole laundry thing really isn't working out for us. We'll get it right someday.

To my readers: 3:AM Kisses was one of the best times I've had writing, and I'm thrilled to get to share it with all of you. I love all of your feedback, your comments, the time you take to let me know how you feel about my novels. I really do wish you could know just how much you mean to me. Big hugs to one and all!

To my sweet betas, proofreaders, and rockin' editor, thank you once again for putting up with my insane antics which often results in multiple Facebook messages, texts, and numerous and sometimes disturbing emails. Delphina Miyares, thank you for saving me from pulling my hair out! As always your input changed the course of many a chapter. BIG thank you for saving me again!

Christina Kendler, you are worth your weight in gold! Thank you for pulling me from the clutches of ultimate disaster. Every time I see a peacock, I think of you! You're just as beautiful inside and out. Thank you for taking the time out of your crazy busy life to help me. It really does mean everything to me.

To Rachel Tsoumbakos, thank you for pulling me out of a pickle and lending me your sweet eyes! You are incredible at what you do. I so appreciate it. And, to my rock star editor, Sarah Freese. There aren't enough Wicked Whoopies in the world to say thank you, but I'll keep trying. You're amazing girl, and you know it. Ready for another book?

And a big giant thank you to Regina Wamba and her gorgeous cover models, Dylan Prichard and Julia Plan. The three of you created magic together. The cover love for this book was through the roof, and it was all because of you. Regina thank you for putting up with me. I'm so glad I didn't scare you off, but I'm sure I came this close. You rocked the cover like I knew you would. Big hugs and kisses for that!

To Him who sits on the throne—each day I smile with peace in my heart because I am forgiven. I owe you everything.

About the Author

Addison Moore is a *New York Times*, *USA Today*, and *Wall Street Journal* bestselling author who writes contemporary and paranormal romance. Her work has been featured in *Cosmopolitan* magazine. Previously she worked for nearly a decade as a therapist on a locked psychiatric unit. She resides with her husband, four wonderful children, and two dogs on the West Coast where she eats too much chocolate and stays up way too late. When she's not writing, she's reading.

Please visit her at:
http://addisonmoorewrites.blogspot.com
Facebook: Addison Moore Author
Twitter: @AddisonMoore
Instagram: http://instagram.com/authoraddisonmoore